PAINT BY NUMBER

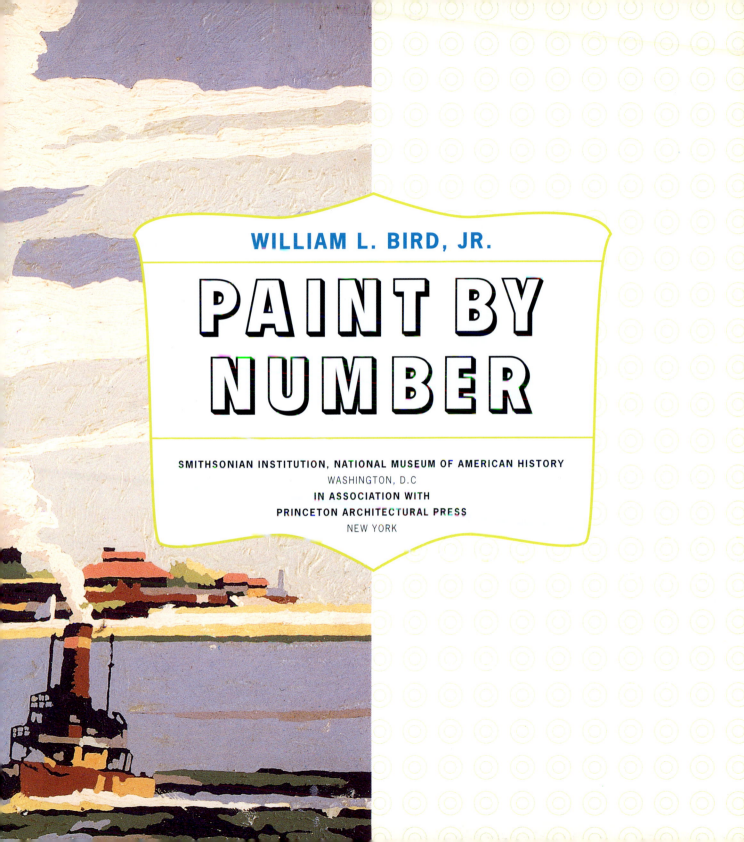

WILLIAM L. BIRD, JR.

PAINT BY NUMBER

SMITHSONIAN INSTITUTION, NATIONAL MUSEUM OF AMERICAN HISTORY
WASHINGTON, D.C
IN ASSOCIATION WITH
PRINCETON ARCHITECTURAL PRESS
NEW YORK

PUBLISHED BY
Princeton Architectural Press
37 East Seventh Street
New York, NY 10003

For a catalog of books published by Princeton Architectural Press,
call toll free 800.722.6657 or visit www.papress.com.

EDITOR/PROJECT COORDINATOR: Jennifer Thompson
BOOK DESIGN: Sara E. Stemen
COVER DESIGN: Deb Wood

SPECIAL THANKS: Nettie Aljian, Ann Alter, Amanda Atkins, Nicola Bednarek, Jan Cigliano, Jane Garvie, Mia Ihara, Clare Jacobson, Mark Lamster, Anne Nitschke, Lottchen Shivers, Tess Taylor, Jennifer Thompson, and Deb Wood of Princeton Architectural Press

–Kevin C. Lippert, publisher

PRINTED IN HONG KONG

LIBRARY OF CONGRESS CATALOGING-IN-PUBLICATION DATA
Bird, William L.
    Paint by number / by William L. Bird.
        p. cm.
    ISBN 1-56898-282-8
    1. Paint-by-numbers—United States—History. 2. Paint-by-numbers—
    United States—Social aspects. 3. Painting—Technique. I. Title.
    ND1471.5 .B57 2001
    306.4'7—dc21   00-011279

CONTENTS

Paint by Number revisits a period in national life and culture in which issues of contention were less between Left and Right, than High and Low. The exhibit points up the democratizing features of the mass market for hobbies and crafts that put paint brushes into the hands of millions who later became the patrons of museums and other centers of cultural activity in the decades after the Second World War.

Americans seldom agree in matters of taste. When paint by number arrived as a popular pastime in the early Fifties, it opened a cultural fissure that has never closed. The hobby, like its paintings, raises curious eyebrows even today. The enormous popularity of paint by number generated discussions of taste among consumers and critics alike. For the former, the paintings became a visual experience in the home. For the latter, the process became a metaphor for the mechanization of culture. Since that time, paint by number has become a symbol of the extension of mass culture's popular methods and predictable effects throughout social and political life.

Spencer R. Crew
Director
National Museum of American History

INTRODUCTION

ABOVE AND OPPOSITE, BACKGROUND:
WINTER SNOW. Test painting and printed line art

OPPOSITE, MARGIN:
A mainstay in the children's craft market: the Tom Sawyer paint set,
c. 1955, and alphabetically-keyed paint set card, c. 1923

Paint by Number revisits the popular hobby from the vantage point of the artists and entrepreneurs who created the paint kits, the critics who reviled them, and the consumers who willingly filled them in and hung them in their homes. The exhibit dramatizes the cultural fault line coursing beneath the construction of elite and popular culture in postwar America, and in the end suggests that the participatory ideal of paint by number—realized primarily by individuals who had never before held a paint brush—affirmed in a very American way, the cultural value of art.

Though keyed paint sets had been marketed for children since the Twenties—exemplified by the "Tom Sawyer" alphabetically-keyed watercolor paint set—not until the early Fifties did paint by number become an adult metaphor for the commercialization and mechanization of culture. In 1954, the hobby's critics ruefully noted that more "number paintings" hung in Americans' homes than did original works of art. The previous year the hobby industry had realized sales of $80 million retail, at an average price of $2.50 for a kit with two to three canvases and a palette varying from 8 to 90 colors. Some thirty companies entered the field, dominated by three major producers who divided up

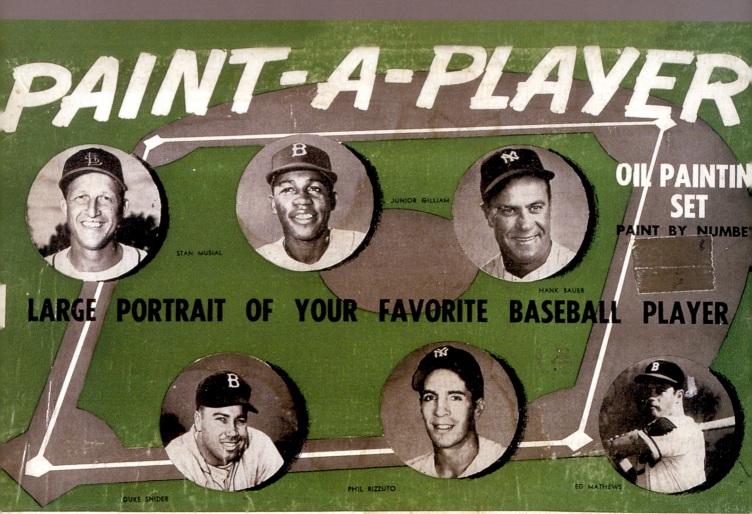

ABOVE: Paint-a-Player

OPPOSITE: Manufacturers of keyed paint sets tapped youthful enthusiasm for portraits of sports figures. Baseball's Duke Snider (**TOP LEFT**) and Carl Erskine (**TOP RIGHT**) took on the nicotine patina of the Brooklyn bar and restaurant in which they hung, where sports entertainment was "on tap."

TOP LEFT: Duke Snider, Brooklyn Dodgers, outfielder; **TOP RIGHT:** Carl Erskine, Brooklyn Dodgers, pitcher; **BOTTOM LEFT:** Bob Lemon, Cleveland Indians, pitcher; **BOTTOM CENTER:** Bobby Avila, Cleveland Indians, pitcher; **BOTTOM RIGHT:** Larry Doby, Cleveland Indians, outfielder

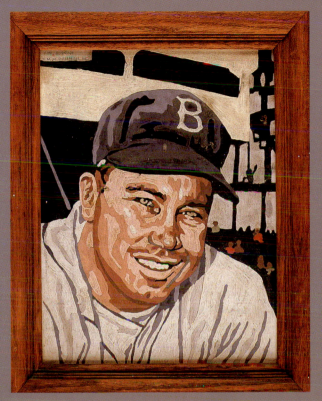
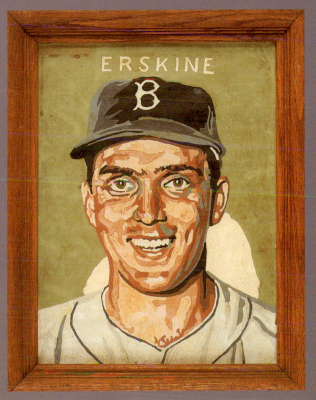

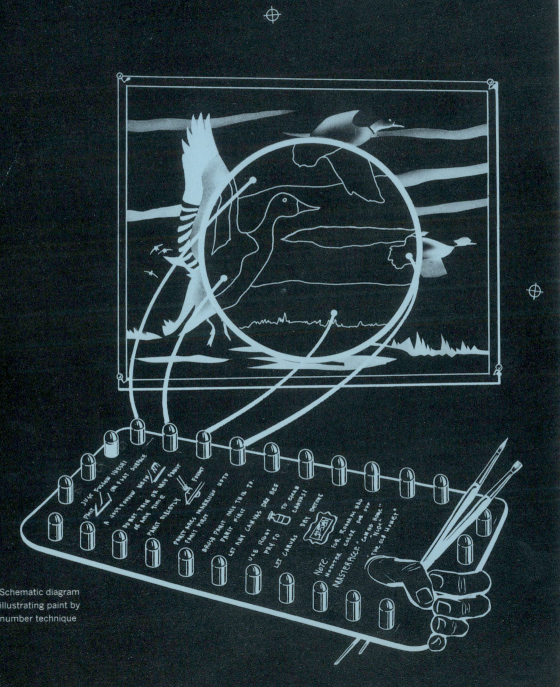

Schematic diagram
illustrating paint by
number technique

80% of the market: the Palmer Show Card Paint Company of Detroit; Picture Craft Company of Decatur, IL; and Master Artists Materials, Inc. of Brooklyn.[1] Palmer Paint, the most prolific merchandiser of the three, offered an abstract still life, traditional land- and seascapes, horses and pets, religious subjects, and a "Masterpiece" line including da Vinci's *Last Supper*. Since that time, the expression "by the numbers" has become a pejorative for culture's most formulaic products, derived from models of popular effect, leaving little to chance.

What is striking about paint by number's popularity is the speed with which it became a vessel for anxieties about mass culture's intrusion into the well-cultured world of taste and social class. Paint by number's ready-made appeal fit the preconceptions of the mass culture critique, which criticized the stock characteristics of "standardization, stereotypy, conservatism, mendacity, manipulated consumer goods."[2] The denunciation of paint by number became a sport among social critics preoccupied with the raw edge of suburbia, where mass culture seemed most at home with the jerry-built entropy of supermarket sad hearts, tract houses, picture windows, and pink

LEFT:
Twin Scotty
paint kit

RIGHT:
Masterpiece
oil painting set

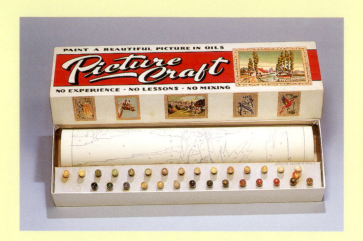

ABOVE LEFT:
Picture Craft Company kit, c. 1949–1955. A manufacturer of artist's supplies dating to the Thirties, the Picture Craft Company began producing paint by number kits in 1949. The company's early kits were devised by Royce Caron, a commercial artist who began his career in Sault Ste. Marie, Michigan, and whose commissions there included a painting for the chapel of the local Salvation Army. Caron reportedly developed his paint by number idea during the Second World War, as a therapeutic pastime for servicemen confined to hospital. An acquaintance later recalled that Caron targeted his kits for the "average person, needing not a lot of talent." Lacking the financing to market the idea, not until moving to Decatur, Illinois, and later Springfield, Illinois, did Caron market kits through Picture Craft. Early Picture Craft paint by number subjects included Mountain Road, Columbia Jay, and military subjects such as naval destroyers and PT boats.[3]

ABOVE RIGHT: MOUNTAIN ROAD

RIGHT: COLUMBIA JAY. After Audubon

OPPOSITE: DESERT LANDSCAPE

lampshades.[4] The unchecked popularity of number painting threatened artistic values, just as the parlor lithograph of an earlier day had leavened the cultural authority of art; paradoxically, the mechanical processes of reproduction made art more accessible.[5]

As the well-oiled bric-a-brac of Victorian domesticity, and the traditional markers of breeding and background, receded in significance, cultural critics determined that social class had become a matter of what one did with his or her "New Leisure," since it was now thought that everyone had an abundance of it. While hobbyists paid little attention to critics who urged the wise use of leisure, the doing of paint by number, the framing of the finished canvas, and its display in the home offered an outlet for a contrarian statement of sorts. Gestures included signing or initialing completed paintings, or entering them as original work in amateur art contests. In other quarters the juxtaposition of paint by number with the apparatus of fine art made light of the authority of experts, who in this discourse enjoyed every advantage except being in on the joke.

Cutting across the fields of mass media, leisure and recreation, home economics and art education, *Paint by Number* pictures the phenomenon in the full flower of Fifties

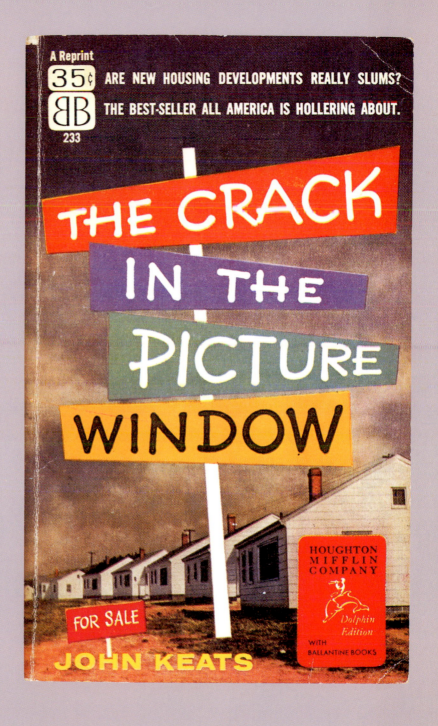

THE CRACK IN
THE PICTURE
WINDOW, 1956

leisure, pitting enthusiastic hobbyists against cold water-throwing critics whose positions may be summarized as "more" and "morons":

> I know I'm not much of an artist and never will be. I've tried in vain repeatedly to draw or paint something recognizable. With envy I study the pictures in *American Artist*, even those by your amateurs. But why oh why didn't you or somebody else tell me before this how much fun is to use these wonderful 'paint by number' sets?[6]

> I don't know what America is coming to when thousands of people, many of them adults, are willing to be regimented into brushing paint on a jig-saw miscellany of dictated shapes and all by rote. Can't you rescue some of these souls—or should I say 'morons'?—before they are lost forever? Can't you make them see that such an exercise is stifling to say the least—that the only real satisfaction in painting comes from creating something which is one's own?[7]

The exhibit idea has been shaped by the pioneering work of sociologist Herbert J. Gans, who declared that everyone has the right to the culture that they prefer, whether it may be perceived as élite or popular. It draws from the recent work of historians Lawrence W. Levine, T. J. Jackson Lears, Michael Kammen, and others, who note that the distinctions of élite and popular are themselves active social constructions; and it extends the work of art historian Karal Ann Marling (who has described paint by number as the ultimate "masterpiece" of Fifties recreation) in considering what people actually like to look at.[8]

In an effort to capture reminiscences about the paint by number hobby, the exhibit has applied the apparatus of audience research to the problem of evidence, tapping the memories of those individuals who became familiar with the paint kits and paintings at the height of their popularity. Contemporary descriptions of the hobby by its creators and critics who left written records have been weighed with reminiscences about the hobby's personal meaning and effect, good, bad, but never indifferent in regard to the distinctions of art and craft.[9]

LEFT: Wall clock

RIGHT: More time for this. Detroit Edison, c. 1955. An icon by 1955, paint by number was seen as one of the leisure time benefits of Total Electric living.

INDIAN CHIEF
AND INDIAN
PRINCESS.
Rendered with
commercial rather
than ethnographic
intent, paint by
number Indian
portraits drew
upon the romantic
past of travel
and tourism
illustration.

At the outset it should be noted that paint by number is not art. It is the contention of this exhibit that the charge of "not art" levied against the hobby functioned as a kind of club fashioned by middle and upper-class critics with which to rough up the legitimate aspirations of middle to lower-class hobbyists who were fully aware of paint by number's limitations. While the popularity of "number painting" registered at all levels of society, the persistent charge of "not art," especially of the "they don't know what they're doing" kind will be described here as a social construction. Simply stated, hobby kits, like paint by number, functioned as a compromise between genuine creativity and the responsibilities of homemaking and earning a living. The real art began the moment the hobbyist ignored outlines to blend adjacent colors, added or dropped a detail, or elaborated upon a theme by extending the composition onto the frame. By doing what art was not supposed to be, one could learn what it was.

ABOVE LEFT:
BUDDHA

ABOVE RIGHT:
ORIENTAL
SHRINE

OPPOSITE:
JUDAICA

OVERLEAF:
CHRIST IN
GETHSEMANE

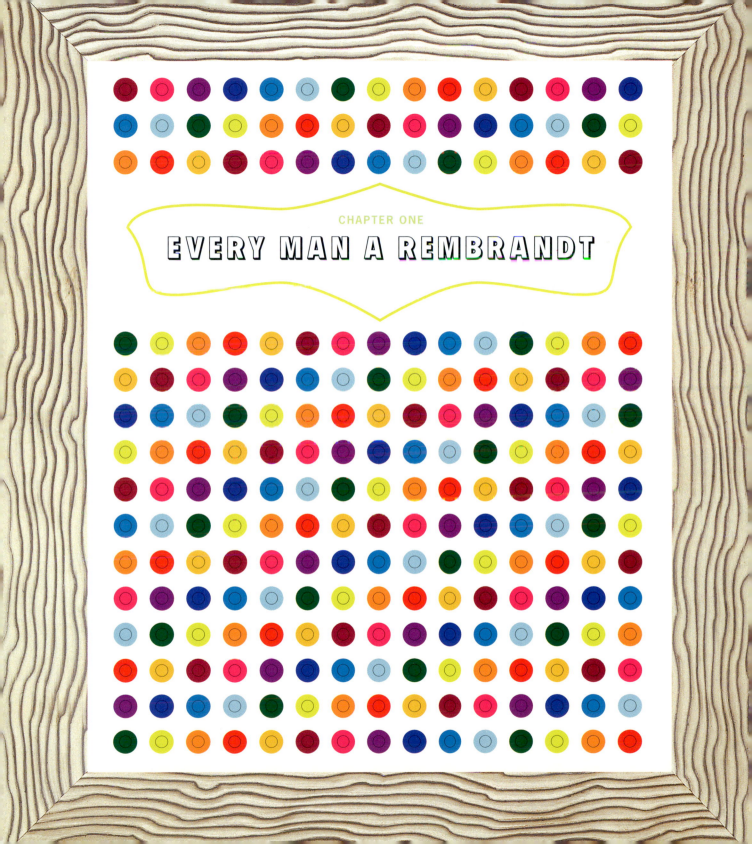

CHAPTER ONE

EVERY MAN A REMBRANDT

The paint by number phenomenon began in the Fall of 1952 when a now unknown San Francisco Bay area hobbyist entered a Craft Master still life in a local amateur art contest. The painting, a melange of faux-cubist forms entitled *Abstract No. One*, won third prize. Not until the prizes were awarded was *Abstract No. One* revealed to be the product of a paint by number kit. The errant award elicited no comment from the contest's judges, who were reported to be too embarrassed to talk about it.[1]

Rendered in a climate of both compulsive consumption and criticism of the product as "art," the paint by number phenomenon was appropriately enough a Detroit product. The Palmer Show Card Paint Company, the manufacturer of *Abstract No. One* and the era's leading merchandiser of paint by number kits, drew its assembly line techniques, as well as its top management, from the ranks of the local auto industry. Palmer

Paint Company owner and president Max S. Klein and art department head Dan Robbins, the creator of *Abstract No. One*, had each labored in the orbit of General Motors.

Klein, a graduate chemist, had edited technical manuals for Fisher Body during the Second World War. After the war, Klein realized his desire for independence unattainable in the middling ranks of the world's largest automaker. In a 1953 interview published in *Time* magazine Klein recalled, "Gee whiz, it got terrible being stuck there at General Motors. I began to look around for a way out." The way out was the tiny Palmer Show Card Paint Company.[2] Founded in 1932, Palmer Paint specialized in the manufacture of tempera powders sold in bulk to commercial sign painters. Purchasing the company in 1945, Klein set out to expand the wholesale market for Palmer paint. Applying his training in chemistry to the manufacture of paint, and business acumen emphasizing customer relations in the manner of his previous employer, Klein won contracts with the City of Philadelphia Board of Education and the New York Board of Education.[3] Klein also marketed flesh-tone mannikin paint, and special "ice paint" that lined the hockey rinks and decorated the ice skating shows of the Midwest. Despite its

THE BUMBLEBEE CANNOT FLY

According to recognized aerotechnical tests, the bumblebee cannot fly because of the shape and weight of his body in relation to the total wing area.

BUT, the bumblebee doesn't know this, so he goes ahead and flies anyway.

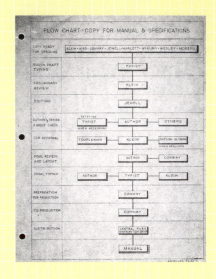

LEFT: THE BUMBLEBEE CANNOT FLY. c. 1943. Klein saved GM incentive posters among his personal papers.

TOP RIGHT: Flow Chart—Copy for Manual & Specifications. During the Second World War Klein rose to an executive position at GM's Fisher Body as an editor of technical manuals used to iron out production bugs with aircraft sub-assembly contractors.

BOTTOM RIGHT: GOOD BUSINESS. 1944

Dan Robbins painting diorama figures for General Motors's Motorama, 1946.

Barnumesque name, "ice paint" had no particular characteristic, with the exception that it was Palmer paint applied to ice.

In 1949 Klein hired artist Dan Robbins to design consumer packages for Palmer's fledgling retail trade in fingerpaint and "L'il Abner" figurine painting sets. Robbins began his career as a free lance artist with the H. B. Stubbs Co., a GM subcontractor then producing the automaker's "Motorama" exhibit at Chicago's Museum of Science and Industry. For a brief period before joining Klein at Palmer Paint, Robbins worked for the Chart and Art Department of the Chevrolet Central office in Detroit, making brush and pen lettering for flip charts and other motivational aids.

Robbins's vocational education and wartime experience were central to the marketing of paint by number. A 1943 graduate of Detroit's Cass Technical High School, Robbins had enlisted in the Army Corps of Engineers at the age of 18. Recalling the experience years later, Robbins noted that he had expected to design and install aerial camouflage for stateside war plants. Instead, he found himself on Utah beach on D-Day plus three. For the war's duration Robbins scouted the infrastructure of liberated roads

ABOVE: APRIL IN PARIS

RIGHT: Display stand with Craft Master Oil
Painting Set

and bridges needed to sustain advancing Allied supply lines. Assigned to the Allied head-quarters staff, Robbins became acquainted with the French historical and cultural monuments, which remained intact with their protective measures still much in evidence. Robbins later recalled that the French had sandbagged Notre Dame, Chartres, and Rheims to their gargoyles, and removed their fabled windows for safekeeping. Then, of course, there was the soldiers' Montmartre and the Moulin Rouge. Such memories inspired the Parisian streetscapes of the Palmer line and those of its competitors, who developed parallel catalogues of paint by number subjects in the Fifties.

 While the Second World War opened new vistas and visual experiences from which to draw in peacetime, a recollection from Robbins's art student days at Cass Tech became the immediate inspiration for Palmer Paint's marketing of paint by number. What is striking about paint by number's development as a pastime for adults, with subjects for adult tastes, rolled canvases, and oil paints, is that the concept simultaneously recommended itself to Royce Caron at Picture Craft and Dan Robbins at Palmer Paint. Until their respective kit lines rose to prominence in the early 1950s, each worked in apparent ignorance of the other.

LEFT:
NOTRE DAME

RIGHT:
EIFFEL TOWER

OVERLEAF,
LEFT:
PARISIAN NEWS
VENDOR

OVERLEAF,
RIGHT:
PARISIAN
FLOWER SALES

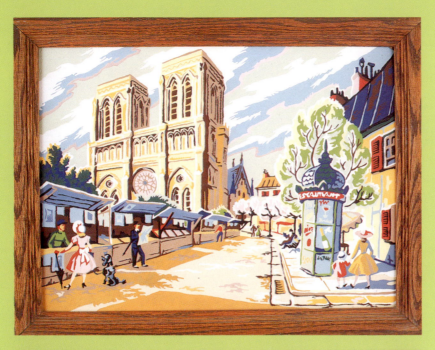

ABOVE: NOTRE DAME

LEFT: ARC DE TRIOMPHE

SUBURB DE PARIS

Klein, Robbins and Palmer Paint soon enjoyed an advantage in that market. Robbins legitimately drew his inspiration from a story about Leonardo da Vinci he remembered from vocational art class at Cass Tech. Years later, while playing with a Palmer washable paint set (for which he was designing more subjects), Robbins recalled that da Vinci had assigned numbered portions of paintings to his assistants to complete. Robbins wondered if da Vinci's method might be applied to a paint set for adults. The idea was to put brushes in the hands of hobbyists unfamiliar with the apparatus of art and the painterly processes of composition.[4]

Though critics would come to castigate the wild popularity of "number painting" in the coming years, the paint by number concept was of a piece with contemporary visual instruction. As art historian David Deichter notes, the ideology of visual instruction was distinguished by "a singularly rational approach to teaching unprecedented numbers of students the skills of pictorial organization and commercial design...united with a still romantic belief in the inherent benevolence of art and science."[5] Though the underlying commercial and scientific ethos of postwar visual instruction had special con-

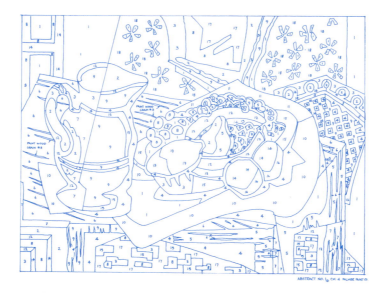

Line art for ABSTRACT NO. ONE. Robbins's schematic of differentiated color blocks, keyed to a 22-color palette.

sequence for the Pop Art movement of the Sixties, its first and most popular product of consequence was the paint by number kit of the Fifties.

Robbins took the concept to Klein, who, upon hearing it, asked to see a sample. Considering what an adult hobbyist might enjoy in the way of a composition, Robbins painted *Abstract No. One*, broke it into differentiated color blocks, and keyed each to a palette. Though Klein's reaction to abstract subject matter was an unqualified "I hate it," *Abstract No. One* became one of Palmer's earliest paint by number subjects.[6] Though *Abstract No. One* would win at least one prize from amateur art contest judges unfamiliar with the process, as a subject it did not appeal to hobbyists for whom the process mattered less than the finished product.[7] Thereafter, Robbins and Klein predicated paint by number's success upon more representational still lifes, land and seascapes, and figure studies. Each began with the undulating pattern of keyed color blocks and ended with *Fishermen*, *Mt. Matterhorn*, *Latin Figures*, and *The Bullfighter*.

Having settled upon an initial run of representational subjects, Klein set out to move the product by merchandising the process. Through his contacts with S. S. Kresge

LEFT:
LATIN FIGURES
RIGHT: THE
BULLFIGHTER

in Detroit, Klein arranged for a test. Planning four initial subjects, Palmer Paint first produced *Fishermen* and *The Bullfighter*, and shipped them to Kresge. In the rush to market, however, production workers inadvertently switched the kits' palettes, with uniformly disastrous results. Kresge consumers scrupulously applied the enclosed palette to the accompanying canvas, withholding judgment until filling in the last color block. *The Bullfighter*, Robbins recalled, "was wearing brown tights, waving a blue cape and fighting a green bull." The *Fishermen* had a "red sky, yellow water and pink boats." Consumers seeking refunds returned their strange paintings to Kresge.[8]

Success came the following March, at the 1951 New York Toy Fair. Klein and Robbins arrived in style from Detroit in a Chrysler New Yorker that Klein had contracted to deliver to its new owner in Brooklyn, though not before packing the car with several hundred Craft Master sets for a demonstration at Macy's. Leaving nothing to chance, Klein salted the demonstration with cash-bearing friends and acquaintances who initiated a run on the store's stock. By the time it was over, Robbins wondered if Klein's ruse had been the deciding factor, or if Macy's customers truly had been taken with the paint by

You'll Want to Paint them All
THERE IS A COMPLETE ASSORTMENT OF
BEAUTIFUL SUBJECTS FOR EVERYONE TO ENJOY

FISHERMEN—Here is dynamic drama!! Who but the dauntless toilers of the sea are privileged to behold the constantly changing kaleidoscope of color about them as they taste the tang of salt air and pit their strength and courage against their beloved adversary.

A few daubs of your brush and all the drama, magnificence and restlessness of the sea are suddenly created. "Impossible", you will say, and yet there before your unbelieving eyes you see captured on canvas this saga of the sea.

Subject No. CM-1

MARINE FANTASY—You won't believe that a few simple strokes of your brush can possibly create such beauty, gracefulness and exciting colors! As this fantastic world unfolds, you feel the urge to catch the underwater enchantment as you explore the mysteries of the ocean's uncharted depths.

Leave humdrum and cares behind. Using paint, brush and canvas, project yourself into this Marine Fantasy where time and space remain suspended and nature rules supreme.

Subject No. CM-2

MT. MATTERHORN—Plunge your brush into the numbered colors and daub the canvas before you with careless strokes . . . Easy isn't it . . . Behold!! Magically appears the mighty majestic Matterhorn crowned with a shimmering, glistening coat of virgin snow.

Continue with the rich warm brown tones used to capture the simple life of the shepherd who travels the narrow twisting trails dotted with rustic shelters.

Centuries of change and progress come and go, but the majestic simplicity of the Matterhorn, emerging from the canvas with each successive stroke of your brush, remains unchanged; an incomparable monument of natural creation.

Subject No. CM-3

ABSTRACT # ONE—"Resist me if you can", shouts this composition of esthetic expression. Truly this is art in its purest form!

It's so easy to do and yet so amazing to watch the paint flow freely from your brush becoming the pure rich color of fruit . . . its rich lusciousness emphasized by a contrasting dark outline. Notice how the background of warm yet pleasing red embraces the subject. Strength and drama are added by the diagonal line that separates the pitcher into forms of light and dark. A subdued background, made interesting by its varying pattern, lends a certain charm, and the suggestion of a linoleum floor, an ornamented chair and a battered kitchen table create an impression that is indeed nostalgic.

Subject No. CM-4

LATIN FIGURES—Color . . . Vivid and profuse . . . Rich Archipelago Red contrasted with cool refreshing Emerauld Green, becomes a beautiful natural setting against the background of a cloudless infinitely blue sky.

Bare brown feet tread noiselessly through the ochre colored dust of the picturesque mud-walled village as morning chores are begun in this atmosphere of artistic inspiration.

Be Fearless and Bold! . . . for the uneven strokes of your brush will lend character and mood to this sunlit story in color.

Subject No. CM-5

THE BULLFIGHTER—Stand aside you weaklings!! . . . for here the Red on your paint brush turns magically into flowing blood as the climax of Matador versus Bull draws near.

As your numbered colors bring life and drama to your canvas, the excitement of this moment is without parallel for here is tension, lust and fury. Yes, this dramatic painting of action in the sunlit arena will be yours to relive time and again as it lends romance and color to its surroundings.

Subject No. CM-6

You'll want to paint them all. Palmer's initial run of Craft Master painting subjects ranged from the representational to the abstract.

number idea. Perhaps both. In the short term, it didn't matter. The sets had flown off the shelf, and Macy's wanted more.

Returning to Detroit, Klein and Robbins plotted additional subjects for the fledgling Craft Master line, and began to hire local artists to develop them. Robbins's first find was Adam Grant, a figural artist who labored on the assembly line at Ford's River Rouge auto plant. A Polish Catholic born Adam Grochowski, Grant had immigrated to the United States after the Second World War. Grant's mother was a school teacher, his father a physician who painted meticulous replicas of Old Masters. As a youth, Grant was given watercolors, never oils, with which to paint. At the age of seventeen his talent for illustration literally saved his life. Caught in the Nazi roundup of Polish civilians after the Battle of Stalingrad, Grant was sent to concentration camps at Auschwitz and Mauthausen. At Mauthausen the brutal regimen of slave labor and starvation spelled certain death. Though Grant later recalled that it was dangerous to volunteer for anything, he responded to his captors' offer of an extra bowl of soup when a call went out through the camp for an artist. As a test Grant was given ten minutes to sketch

RIGHT: Adam Grochowski. BOHRER. Watercolor on paper. 1944. 27.5 x 19 cm. Courtesy of the Auschwitz-Birkenau Museum. The Polish translation of "Bohrer" is "The Driller." Believed to have been painted before Mauthausen's liberation in 1945, this composition is remarkable for its identification of a prisoner laborer, foreground.

BELOW, LEFT: Shift change at Ford's River Rouge plant, c. 1950

BELOW, RIGHT: Artist Adam Grant. Grant specialized in figure studies (BALLET INTERMISSION, THE LOVE BALLET, THE LAST SUPPER, THE RED SHOES) and landscapes with figures (APRIL IN PARIS).

LEFT:
THE RED SHOES

RIGHT:
BALLET
INTERMISSION

a portrait of the camp commandant. Another unforgettable assignment was to paint a mural of fruit on the wall of the prison dining room. Grant never learned if the mural was a psychological ploy or a spur-of-the-moment decision on the part of his captors. Recognized as the camp artist, Grant was given duties around the barracks, and paid in cigarettes for birthday cards drawn up for exchange among prison block leaders and guards and their families and girlfriends. "Roses and butterflies," he recalled, "for men who could have killed me at any time."[9]

With the hiring of artists Robbins now became a functional manager, culling the line, ordering new subjects, and supervising production. Robbins organized the Palmer Paint art department along lines inspired by Walt Disney's animation unit. By 1953, 35 artists worked on the Craft Master line. In another location, some 30 more were devoted to a start up venture in "Personal Portraits."

Palmer artists specialized in landscapes, landscapes with figures, seascapes, still lifes, flowers, religious studies, and animals and pets, typically puppies and kittens. An artist specializing in a particular subject was expected to paint it in a variety of sizes to fit

ABOVE:
THE LAST SUPPER.
Grant's rendering of
da Vinci's LAST
SUPPER remains the
hobby's most popular
subject.

RIGHT:
THE LOVE BALLET

RIGHT: Artist Wasgin Havenitian, who specialized in floral still life.

BELOW: Wasgin Havenitian (attributed), BLOSSOM TIME line art and palette; Wasgin Havenitian (attributed), BLOSSOM TIME

OPPOSITE; The Palmer Paint Company art department at Woodward and Canfield in downtown Detroit, 1953. From left to right: Millie Forgash (foreground, seated), Ted Topolski (standing), Peggy Brennan (obscured), Ed Lazar (background, seated), Lenord d'Aoust (seated), unknown (seated), Dick Hess (background, standing), Herb Miller (background, standing), Adam Grochowski (later Grant, foreground, seated), unknown, unknown.

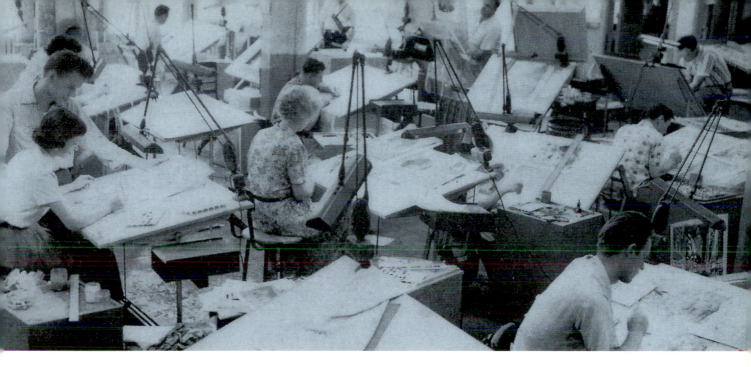

standard-size frames (from 8" x 10" to 24" x 36"), using a predetermined number of colors (ranging from 8 to 90 colors in the largest sets). Artists could specify specially mixed colors, if needed.

The process of building a picture began with creation of a painting, developed with a "high degree" of artistry. The picture subject was then broken down into component color blocks, resulting in a schematic drawing keyed to a palette.[10] The undulating pattern of differentiated color blocks was tested and retested to ensure that anyone with the patience to complete the painting would achieve the same result—while earning the distinction of having painted it oneself.

Palmer Paint's development of painting subjects owed nothing to the nuances of highly focused audience research available in our Nielsen ratings age, other than reading the mail received at company headquarters from hobbyists inquiring about pictures of landscapes, figures, flowers, and pets. After *Abstract No. One*, which proved to be unpopular, the vetting of painting subject matter proceeded along the representational lines delivered by the postman. The informal vetting process was flexible enough to

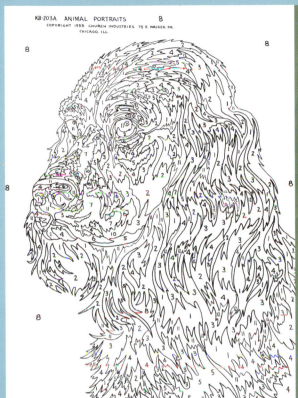

ABOVE LEFT: ANIMAL PORTRAITS (spaniel). Printed line art

ABOVE RIGHT: Richard Hess. ANIMAL PORTRAITS (spaniel). Oil paint on posterboard and celluloid. Palmer Paint Co. for Church Industries, Inc.

OPPOSITE, TOP LEFT: Palmer Paint art department director Dan Robbins pictured with "Personal Portrait" paintings, c. 1954

OPPOSITE, TOP RIGHT: Artist Herb Miller

OPPOSITE, BOTTOM LEFT: Artist Ed Lazar

OPPOSITE, BOTTOM RIGHT: Artist Millie Forgash, inking a harbor scene. In the background, her design for the "crown" palette included in Palmer Paint's "Queen Elizabeth" portrait set, 1953.

LEFT:
BEFORE
THE WIND

RIGHT:
ALONG
THE ROAD

accommodate the quirky taste of Max Klein, Palmer's owner-operator, and chief marketer. Dan Robbins later recalled that once the program of representational subject matter was put in place, Klein seldom expressed an interest in kit subjects other than to specify his preference for the color red, although this often meant adding an additional color to the kit's palette. Palmer Paint subjects typically featured red details, such as the ship's flag in *Before the Wind*. Whether by chance or design, small red details found their way into the work of Palmer Paint's competitors, such as the distant chimney pictured in Craftint Company's *Along the Road*.

If Robbins' model of production was Disney, Klein's was General Motors. Klein and company proceeded to rationalize a "family" of products, developing a hierarchical pricing scheme like that of General Motors, which in the Twenties promoted "a car for every purse and purpose."

In an effort to broaden the appeal of the hobby among all age groups, Palmer developed a "1-2-3" paint set. Describing it as "quick and easy to paint" and "maintain[ing] a high quality canvas structure," Palmer marketed the "1-2-3" set for children

RIGHT:
Dan Robbins, package prototype, "1-2-3" paint set, 1953

BELOW:
A paint set for every purse and purpose

oil painting set
"1,2,3"
Easy
with 2 mounted 8"x10 pictures
A beautiful oil painting the first time you try!...just follow the numbers

ABOVE: Photomural demonstration

LEFT: SLEIGH RIDE

and adults as a "stepping stone" to more elaborate Craft Master compositions.[11] Describing paint by number's niche in the postwar leisure market, Klein explained: "We have developed a transition item that adds new scope to the hobby business. It's a mass appeal item without limitation of age or sex. Anyone from 8 years up can enjoy this hobby."[12]

As retailers merchandised the painterly process, company officials and hobbyists alike marveled at the end result. Could something that looked so unmechanical be—mechanical?

With requests for kits coming from Canada, Klein established a production facility in Strathroy, Ontario. The Canadian operation assembled kit components, including approved canvas subjects supplied from Detroit. Keeping up with current events, Palmer Paint developed a "Queen Elizabeth" portrait kit. The kit featured a 12 x 16" portrait of the Queen, chiaroscuros of the Queen and Prince Philip, two brushes, and thirty-two capsules filled with pre-mixed oil paints embedded in a golden crown-shaped palette. Palmer Paint successfully marketed the sets in Canada and the United States.[13]

CM-43
BALLET
INTERMISSION

Thoughts of the audience . . . the music . . . the dance . . . are reflected in the faces of the beautiful young ballerinas as they await their dramatic entrance.

CM-37
QUEEN ELIZABETH

The British crown now rests upon the head of a young queen. The nobility of her face tells us she will keep sacred the trust of her people.

CM-43 BALLET INTERMISSION

Philip   Elizabeth

CM-37 QUEEN ELIZABETH

LEFT:
Canadian toy fair display, 1953

RIGHT:
Queen Elizabeth II portrait kit pictured in a Palmer Paint consumer catalog. c. 1954

In 1954 Klein went to England to arrange distribution contracts with Guiterman, Ltd. Klein expanded Palmer Paint's Canadian operation, shipping kit components and designs from there to the continent. Certain subjects popular in America and Canada, however, changed. The English preferred thatched roof cottages in their country scenes, rather than red barns; Picadilly Circus, rather than Times Square; fox and hounds, rather than Davy Crockett. The result, as the line went global, was the gradual relinquishing of Detroit's control of painting subject matter.

In time, Robbins conceded that Palmer Paint had created a far-flung administrative structure "to sustain a fad." When the line expanded from Europe to Japan and Australia, the program was carried out with "not a lot of control" over subject matter, or in the copious attention to detail that had contributed to the line's initial success in America.[14]

As sales took off, *Business Week* magazine noted that "A number of retailers and some of the manufacturers of these kits refer to this process as 'art.' Most do not. As one dealer put it, 'I can tell the difference between money and art. This is

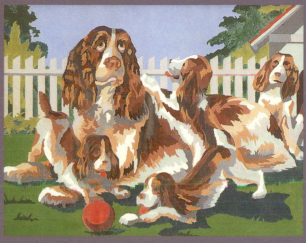

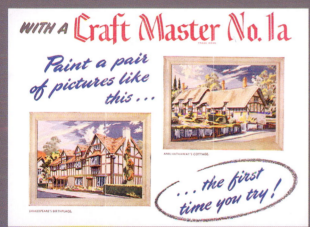

TOP LEFT: Merchandising paint by number at Selfridges Department Store, London

TOP RIGHT: BACK YARD FROLIC

MIDDLE LEFT: "With a Craft Master No. 1a." English advertising brochures featured painting subjects keyed to national tastes, such as Shakespeare's birthplace and Ann Hathaway's cottage.

MIDDLE RIGHT: Guiterman Palmer trade fair display, London. Note the fire screen, lower left.

BOTTOM: FULL CRY

ABOVE LEFT: Italian trade literature

ABOVE MIDDLE: Norwegian trade literature

ABOVE RIGHT: French trade literature. Unlike advertisements elsewhere that presented paint by number as a leisure time activity, French pamphlets emphasized paint by number's "valeur educatif" (educational value).

RIGHT: American trade literature pictured the Craft Master market as an undifferentiated mass.

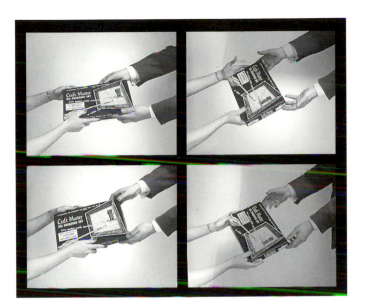 

money.'"[15] One enterprising retailer with a sense of humor packaged a "Paint WITH-OUT Numbers" kit including a blank canvas, a brush and a set of paints. While hobby retailers regarded paint by number as a passing novelty and a "transition item" that turned hobbyists into amateur painters, cultural critics on two continents found nothing to be amused about.

RIGHT: As Palmer Paint's staff artists developed paint kit subjects, they imagined a mythical "Mrs. Murphy" as their loyal customer. This prim fashion model played a comparable role as an idealized consumer in Palmer's advertisements to the trade.

BELOW: Women workers in the Shipping Department, Palmer Paint Company

OPPOSITE: Woolworth Annual Report for 1953. Capitalizing upon paint by number's mounting popularity, leading retailers merchandised paint sets and examples of finished paintings, alongside traditional art supplies.

paint yourself a picture of

PLUS PROFIT

with Craft Master and **masterpiece**

AMERICA'S LEADING OIL PAINTING SETS

- Are you getting your share of the line that leading stores all over the country are calling "the HOTTEST item they've seen in years"?

- It's easy to sell, but best of all... the re-orders are terrific. When you make a sale you start a chain-reaction. Everybody wants one, keep wanting more.

- Get in touch with your jobber today or write or phone us for information.

Palmer Paint, Inc.

31600 WYOMING, DETROIT 20, MICHIGAN
New York, 175 5th Ave. Los Angeles, Box 16690

All necessary art supplies for the amateur, for the student and for the professional are now available in most Woolworth's at budget prices.

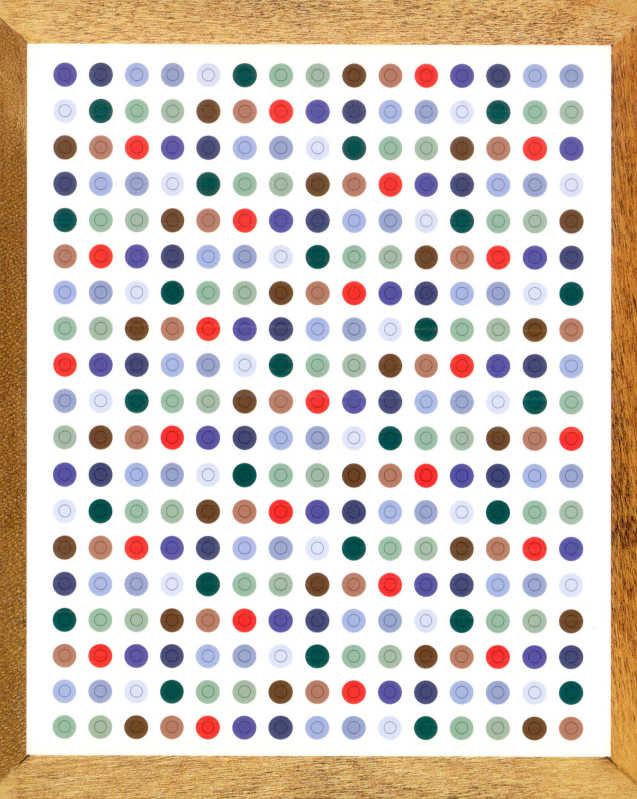

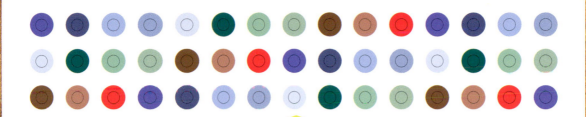

CHAPTER TWO

THE NEW LEISURE

In the edgy prosperity of the Fifties, cultural critics

found Americans ill-equipped for mass culture's siren song. Nowhere was the tilt from class to mass more widely discussed than in essays about the increasing amount of free time enjoyed by the average American, and his apparent willingness to squander it with the products of the busy businessman. As critic Robert Bendiner of the liberal fortnightly *The Reporter* observed, "From the spate of literature on the coming Era of Leisure it is hard to tell whether we are headed for an Elysium of culture that will put the ancient Greeks in the shade or for a hell of mass boredom modified by home carpentry, hi-fi, plush motels, and ping-pong."[1] For its part, the nation's business press heralded the boom market of the newly-leisured masses. *Business Week*, by way of the *New Yorker*, called for a rewriting of Thorstein Veblen's *The Theory of the Leisure Class*. "You used to read a good deal about the leisure class, but something seems to have happened to it. One

OPPOSITE:
JOURNEY
THRU SPACE

What happens to your job—if we get atomic energy to drive our machines?

RIGHT: "What happens to your job,"
1949. The threat of idleness stemming from
technological unemployment lent social
significance to the wise use of free time.

OPPOSITE, RIGHT AND LEFT:
JOURNEY THRU SPACE (small)

thing that may have happened to it is that too many people joined it and the point went out of it."[2]

Cultural critics resumed the heavy lifting of social construction by making class a matter of how one spent his or her "New Leisure." The expression, coined in the late Twenties, had long been applied to the study of free time as the latent consequence of work. As the economically enforced idleness of the Thirties lifted with the rise of unionism, the spread of the five-day work week, and the application of democratic social engineering techniques to almost every aspect of modern life, cultural critics looked to leisure to "furnish an antidote for what is stereotyped and standardized in our present civilization."[3] As late as 1958 sociologist David Riesman noted that "the creation of many jobs which consist of little more than half-attentive dial watching of nearly self-correcting machinery," attached real challenges to leisure. It was better to make the jobs interesting, Riesman suggested, than to saddle the worker's free time with remunerative expectation.[4] Through the Fifties the pursuit of virtuous cultural employment lent social purpose to hobbies and crafts, the do-it-yourself ethos of home repair and decor,

and the enthusiasm for amateur painting inspired by Winston Spencer Churchill, Anna Robertson Moses, and Dwight David Eisenhower.[5]

In 1959 critic Russell Lynes (lately famed for *The Tastemakers*) catalogued the popular pastimes of the "New Leisure" for *Life* magazine. Charting a class system of "Active" and "Sedentary Leisure" (SEE ENDPAPERS), Lynes suggested that traditional markers of distinction such as education, wealth, and breeding, no longer sufficed. The leading indicator of class, Lynes wrote, was how one spent his or her free time.[6]

A dread and fright of leisure betrayed cultural critics' resignation to mass culture's pervasive influence, and businesses' success in colonizing it with a comprehensively-merchandised version of the good life.[7] Critic Harvey Swados, noting historian Arthur Schlesinger, Jr.'s warning that Americans had been "trained to work but not to live," thought that perhaps it was "too late to do anything about it in a missile-maddened, consumption-crazy society premised on lunacy and buttressed by hypocrisy."[8] Anthropologist Margaret Mead, alluding to the Eisenhower administration's emphasis upon mass consumption as the key to national economic prosperity,

Levittown, New York. 1948. Builder William Levitt & Sons brought mass construction techniques to bear upon the postwar housing shortage. Between 1947 and 1951 Levitt & Sons erected 17,447 houses for 50,000 residents on a 6,000 acre tract of land that had once been a Long Island potato farm. The success of Levittown established the pattern of suburban development across the country for Americans who suddenly found themselves with new homes to decorate.

proposed a more fulfilling equilibrium of "work, virtue and leisure."9 Where Mead noted efforts to transform Fifties home life into a "self-rewarding delight," others witnessed the nightmare of conformity. It materialized in densely-built housing tracts springing up outside the metropolitan core, where developers capitalized upon federal home mortgage guarantees, mass construction techniques perfected during the war, widespread automobile ownership, and other consumer durables floated on the bubble of installment credit. As they puzzled out what the good life ought to look like, critics stalked out to the suburbs where they did not have to leave their cars to confirm that this was not it. In an often cited fit of pique, architectural critic Lewis Mumford denounced the suburban development as "a multitude of uniform, unidentifiable houses, lined up inflexibly, at uniform distance, on uniform roads, in a treeless communal waste, inhabited by people of the same class, the same income, the same age group, witnessing the same television programs, eating the same tasteless pre-fabricated foods, from the same freezers, conforming in every outward and inward respect to a common mold."10 If Mumford's indictment seems overdrawn today, it was genuinely felt. *Fortune* editor

Among period
social critics,
pink decorative
accents exempli-
fied the dubious
taste of middle and
lower class home
ownership.

William H. Whyte Jr., for example, parlayed "the pink lampshade in the picture window" into "a sore disappointment to those who dreamed that the emancipation of the
worker might take a more spiritual turn."[11]

The wild popularity of number painting exemplified the breakdown of cultural
standards that had outpaced consumers' capacity to assimilate leisure. Fitting preconceptions of class to diminishing expectations for taste, the hobby had, in a perverse way,
everything going for it. Paint by number demystified art with displays of the painterly
process previously immune to commercial exploitation. Palmer Paint, for example,
deployed gallery-like settings complete with painting demonstrators. For critics, such
displays seemed less a simulation than a violation of art, the "last vestige" of personal
expression in an increasingly impersonal consumer society.[12] The positioning of paint
by number as the "art of creative relaxation" astutely capitalized upon the trend.

The Palmer Paint Company public relations department suggested that theater
owners might be approached to exhibit the finished works of their local patrons. For this
promotion, coincident with the theatrical release of the feature film *Shane*, Detroit's Easy

TOP: Exhibition of paint by number paintings attributed to the Stix, Baer & Fuller department store, St. Louis. The merchandising of paint by number merged the trappings of the art gallery with the display techniques of the modern department store. In this static display, a well-dressed manikin on a hook rug pauses to contemplate a half-completed harbor scene.

BOTTOM LEFT: UNDER THE BRIDGE

BOTTOM RIGHT: ORIENTAL BEAUTY

Text visible within the top image:

"ANYONE CAN DO IT"
THE LADY PAINTING THIS
PICTURE IS NOT A PAINTER
JUST PUT COLOR NO.17 IN SECTION NUMBERED 17 ETC.

ITS AS SIMPLE AS THAT: SURPRISE YOUR FRIENDS
WITH A BEAUTIFUL OIL PAINTING ON CANVAS PAINTED
BY YOU. THEY CAN BE WASHED WITH SOAP AND WATER.
· WHOLESALE DISTRIBUTORS ·
DART GAMES COMPANY INC.,
ROOM 414 BAKER HOTEL OR 2029 MAIN STREET

masterpiece oil painting set
masterpiece oil painting set
JUST FOLLOW THE NUMBERS

Craft Master
OIL PAINTING SETS
12×16 CANVAS $2.50
Take One Home With You

me A Big
Canvas
erpiece
$5.00

TOP: Trade show demonstrator, c. 1953. The simulation of creative experience played a significant role in merchandising the paint by number idea. In this trade show demonstration the exhibitor thoughtfully included a disclaimer: "The lady painting this picture is not a painter."

BOTTOM: Exhibit installation, Michigan Theater, Detroit, 1953

OPPOSITE: SIESTA IN MEXICO

Art Shop exhibited western scenes painted by demonstrators in the lobby of the Michigan Theater. Recommending similar promotional tie-ins to retailers, Palmer Paint cautioned that "Several examples of half-finished art and at least one blank canvas should be used, however, or much of the message is lost."[13]

Giving its paint kits titles such as "Craft Master," "Masterpiece," and "1-2-3," Palmer Paint straddled the market for do-it-yourself projects.[14] The only criteria for success was the ability to recognize numerals, and the patience to apply the premixed paints to their prescribed areas. On this point Palmer Paint was unbending. In promoting local paint by number art contests, company press material urged a stay-within-the-lines aesthetic, noting that "Neatness should be the basis of judging the contest, and pictures should be strictly according to the numbered canvas."[15] Company publicists were just as adamant that paint by number be appreciated as a palliative for, rather than a symptom of, contemporary culture. "Klein saw it," one trade observer reported without a hint of irony, "as an expression of millions of people with latent creative yearnings in a world growing ever more mechanical."[16]

Another big **PROFIT-MAKER** from Palmer Paint!

Toleware

by **Craft Master**

America's only paint-by-numbers Art Metalware with 5 useful decorative sets... in a choice of **6** related picture themes

set shown "Parisian" series

- HEAVY GAUGE METAL
- BRILLIANT PERMAMENT OIL COLORS
- A DECORATIVE HOBBY WITH A **READY MARKET!**

PALMER PAINT SALES
Oak Park 37, Michigan

PRINTED IN U.S.A.
...GHT 1953, PALMER PAINT, INC.

Though the hobby's critics suggested that paint by number had done more to dim the public's perception of art than any other commercial product, the hobby's friends claimed that it raised perceptions where few existed. For example, Nathan Polk of New York City's Polk Hobbies, the nation's largest hobby retailer, attributed the "greatest development" in the hobby market to the use of "number items" in the home. Polk noted that for two or three dollars homemakers could have a little fun, and receive a decorative item in the balance. Polk's salesmen estimated that 10% of paint by number hobbyists graduated to purchases of traditional art supplies for their own compositions, a significant expansion of the business.[17]

The pursuit of painting and paint by number, of course, did not have to be mutually exclusive. The painter Joe Shannon, for example, recalled that his mother, the author of several "Ryderesque romantic seascapes" did both. To his chagrin, Shannon found her one day intently working on a paint by number landscape. "I was appalled and contemptuous. She couldn't have cared less about my reaction. To her it was a diversion like playing solitaire."[18] A survey of visitors at the National Museum of American History taken in January and February 2000 brought forth similar expressions of bemusement about the hobby's

ABOVE LEFT:
Mosette by Craft Master

ABOVE RIGHT:
Tile 'N Frame decorative trivet set

OPPOSITE:
Mosaic pixies of indeterminate manufacture, after Mosette. Crushed stone, ceramic tile, embossed string on composition board with wooden trim

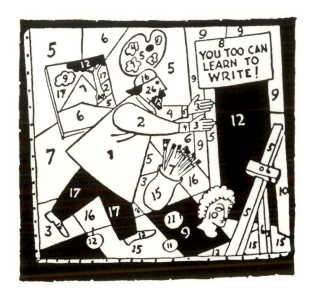

Illustration from "You Too Can Paint." ATLANTIC MONTHLY, June 1955. Down the slippery slope from painting to writing.

place as a family activity that was closer to craft than to art. Respondents recalled childhood gifts of paint by number kits, painting with a brother, sister, parent or grandparent, sometimes finishing, sometimes not, an effort that one respondent described as requiring a level of competence needed to assemble a model airplane.[19] Another respondent recalled a third grade class field trip to Chicago's Art Institute, after which she and her classmates were allowed to choose from several paint by number subjects to paint in class.[20] Not surprisingly, at least one contemporary art educator welcomed the crossover. H. Beam Loomis of the Chicago Art Institute School stated that paint by number "serves the purpose of introducing people to a new and artistic medium of self-expression, and gives them an appreciation of the technique of putting paint on canvas. Many progress to the point—because their imagination is stirred—of trying freehand work on their own." "It may be, Loomis pondered, "that painting by numbers will produce in the next few years serious competition for today's inhabitants of the sacred temples of art."[21]

The acculturation of learning by doing had long been the domain of art education. In mid-nineteenth century America, an "Art Crusade" had coalesced around

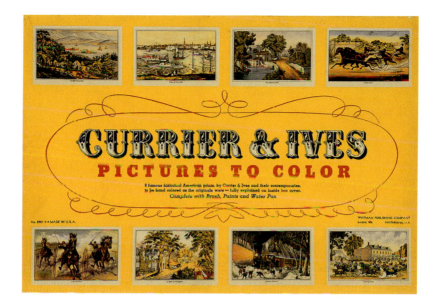

the democratic extension of drawing instruction to mechanics and tradesmen. Just as reading might inculcate a life-long thirst for literature, instruction in rendering rudimentary line forms might whet appetites for art. Popular drawing manuals by John Reubens Smith, Rembrandt Peale, and John Gadsby Chapman offered step-by-step lessons in making outline forms of the human figure, and in advanced stages of instruction, offered tips on composition and perspective. Free-hand was discouraged. If one could learn to read, one could learn to draw.[22] Transmogrifying this truism for a critical mid-twentieth century audience knee-deep in number painting, the *Atlantic Monthly* linked the questionable "You Too Can Paint" to the dubious "You Too Can Learn to Write!"[23]

Paint by number bridged the "visual pleasures" of traditional domestic pastimes with new consumer items that placed a premium upon convenience and ease.[24] The dominant, imaginative, visual experience before television became the focus of attention in the home, paint by number took its place alongside reproducible woodcuts, chromolithographs, photographs, player pianos, plaster casts, magazine illustra-

"You Can Paint A Beautiful Picture."
Easy Art Shop, Detroit. Capitalizing
upon consumer demand for convenience, ease, and paint by number,
this hobby supply store became the
aptly entitled Easy Art Shop.

tions, phonographs, radios, and machine-made furnishings in the New Leisure's bar-
gain bin.[25] Initially shrugged off by mass culture's strident critics as nothing, paint by
number quickly achieved less-then-nothing status in proportion to its popularity
among the public. By this time mass culture's critics had resigned themselves, as historian Bernard De Voto put it, to the mind-numbing products of business' "mendacity,
imbecility, and bilge."[26]

   If critics regarded mass culture's most egregious products as inevitabilities
(defining them as "Kitsch," the product of the historical forces unleashed by the industrial revolution, i.e., mass literacy, boredom, and consumerism[27]), postwar home economists persisted in the belief, if only for professional reasons, that a "discriminating
perception of art quality" among consumers could create a market for sensible furnishings. Home economist Janet K. Smith, for example, argued that,

> Home furnishings...have been made to sell, but not necessarily to be sold to people
> who use judgment or have developed taste in buying. The more one knows, the greater

the capability he has of selecting the best for the money expended and, even more important, of using the selections in such a way as to increase their value for comfort and appearance. An artistic home means more enjoyable living.[28]

The dawning awareness that paint by number had penetrated the home dashed whatever hope home economists may have entertained of harnessing the wiles of the mass market to an aesthetic for living. For not only had number painting become a pastime with which to occupy one's leisure, its decorative side effect tipped the scale of condescension from the politics of doing to the politics of using.

The merchandising of paint by number as an attainable art was nearly as unsettling as its apparent reception in the living room, which begged the question again: Was it art? Addressing the situation in 1954, an unnamed "Dutch art critic" conceded, "There are certainly more numbered paintings hanging in American homes that original works of art." Just getting started, he wrote,

Fancy, you yourself should like to make an oil painting. Such a job you have left to more gifted men, as Rembrandt, Frans Hals, and Van Meegeren. But when you smear a canvas with paint out of a cup of oil paint with a corresponding number, you get an exact reproduction of the original created by some American. You must not forget, that this art of painting has nothing to do with culture... even though it has decorative value for sure, as a work of art, it is worthless.[29]

This critic's assessment of paint by number was notable for its acceptance of the decorative value of the framed painting in the home, but there was more: the assumption that hobbyists who believed paint by numbers was art removed themselves and their paintings from further consideration.

Reminiscences about the hobby gleaned from today's museum visitors suggest that the picture's place is just as actively contested now as then. Citing personal experience with the hobby, respondents described paint by number as "a diversion, but not a self-expression." "It's their art creation," explained one respondent, "and you're helping them finish it." Another, recalling that her mother blended colors "with something like a sponge," explained, "It may not be an original painting but it's definitely art." A second reminisced, "To someone who cannot draw, it's art," while a third qualified the process's limitations as "guided" art. The most compelling evidence of the hobby's lingering effect could be heard in the long pause when survey takers asked the question, "Was it art?" Accounting for lapsed taste in the decades-long pause in the conversation, one respondent observed, "Well, it wasn't in those days."[30]

Art's incredible simulation and the critical reaction to it helped instill a cultural climate in which the signing of a painting or its gallery-like display could be regarded with horror, or amusement, or both. While it lasted the phenomenon was fun indeed. The period's ultimate paint by number display was found not in a department store or a trade fair, but in the Eisenhower White House, where presidential appointment secretary Thomas Edwin Stephens mounted a gallery of paint by number and amateur works by administration officials. Stephens, sometimes confused with Eisenhower portraitist

Thomas Edgar Stephens (both signed their names Thomas E. Stephens), traveled between New York and Washington as the administrative assistant to Secretary of State John Foster Dulles, and later as the chairman of the New York State Republican Party. Residing within two blocks of each other in New York's Greenwich Village in the late Forties, the two Stephens became acquainted over exchanges of mis-delivered mail, and continued their acquaintance into the Fifties through the Eisenhowers. Thomas Edwin Stephens served as Eisenhower's appointment secretary during the General's tenure as Columbia University president in 1950, and worked on behalf of his candidacy for president in 1952. The artist Thomas Edgar Stephens painted a portrait of Mamie Eisenhower during Eisenhower's tenure at Columbia in 1950. Noting Eisenhower's offhand attempt to render a portrait of his wife using the paint left to dry on a palette, Stephens sent a paint set to Eisenhower. Having found his hobby, Eisenhower became a dedicated amateur, working up landscapes in his Columbia penthouse, portraits of Washington and Lincoln in a small room off the elevator on the second floor of the White House, and favorite fishing spots on the enclosed porch of his Gettysburg farm.[31]

At the height of paint by number's popularity in 1954, Stephens—the appointment secretary—hatched the idea of mounting a White House gallery of his own. Not knowing any painters (other than the Stephens who had painted and signed the Eisenhower portrait hanging in his West Wing office), Stephens distributed some twenty Picture Craft number kits to Eisenhower's cabinet secretaries and Oval Office visitors. More than a few assumed that the president himself expected that they paint them, an assumption that the puckish Stephens did little to dispel. Stephens eventually installed the completed paintings in a West Wing corridor outside the Cabinet Room. The "Stephens Collection" featured Picture Craft subjects meticulously executed by Federal Bureau of Investigation director J. Edgar Hoover, Republican National Committee chairman Leonard W. Hall, musician Fred Waring, Governor Harold Stassen, former president Herbert Hoover, special assistant to the president Nelson A. Rockefeller, Secretary of Health, Education, and Welfare Oveta Culp Hobby, U. S. Ambassador to the United Nations Henry Cabot Lodge, singer Ethel Merman, Attorney General Herbert Brownell,

ABOVE: The Stephens Collection, the White House, c. 1956. Installed in a West Wing corridor just outside the Cabinet Room, the Stephens Collection featured paint by number paintings completed by cabinet secretaries and friends of the administration, lithographs of President Eisenhower's amateur paintings given to staff as Christmas gifts, and original amateur work. From left to right: "Thorobred" (paint by number) completed by Secretary of the Interior Douglas McKay; "Black Child," Clare Boothe Luce; "St. Louis Creek, Byers Creek Ranch" (lithograph), Dwight D. Eisenhower; floral still life, unattributed; Lincoln portrait, (lithograph), Eisenhower; "Rocky Mountain Scene," Eisenhower; framed photograph of Eisenhower painting previous scene; Washington portrait (lithograph), Eisenhower; "Deserted Barn" (reproduction), Eisenhower; "Carnival" (paint by number), Mrs. Richard Gulay; "Winter Scene," Rachel Adams; "Columbia Jay" (paint by number), Oveta Culp Hobby; "The Clown - Kelly," Phil Wolf; obscured

LEFT: THE OLD MILL, signed Ethel Merman

Jr., Postmaster General Arthur E. Summerfield, Eisenhower brother and Johns Hopkins University president Milton Eisenhower, and others. Stephens also exhibited the work of the administration's amateur painters, who bypassed the pre-planned canvas route.[32]

Believing that "to want beautiful things is a very human instinct," Nelson A. Rockefeller carried on a life-long fascination with the reproduction of art. As a college student in the early Thirties, Rockefeller became interested in color reproductions of masterworks that he ordered and sold to his fellow students. A lifelong trustee of the Museum of Modern Art and an avid collector of abstract expressionist and pre-Columbian art, Rockefeller in 1978 launched a line of drawings, paintings, sculpture, and furnishings reproduced from his private collection.[33]

The "Stephens Collection" mixed paint by number subjects with original amateur work. Former congresswoman, playwright, author, and ambassador Clare Boothe Luce contributed a watercolor entitled "Black Child." As a young woman Luce had taken classes at Chicago's Art Institute, becoming a "compulsive sketcher" of pastels. Inspired by the example of Winston Churchill, Luce took up painting as a

LEFT:
OLD MISSION
completed by
Nelson Rockefeller.

RIGHT:
BLACK CHILD.
Clare Boothe Luce.
Watercolor

SWISS VILLAGE, completed by
J. Edgar Hoover. The Stephens
Collection featured this Picture
Craft subject meticulously executed
by Federal Bureau of Investigation
director J. Edgar Hoover. Since the
Fifties cultural historians, social
critics, and collectors have come to
appreciate paint by number as the
embodiment of the decade's contra-
dictory aspirations: creativity and
security.[35]

hobby in her mid-fifties.[34] Whether by happenstance or design, Luce's watercolor stood out in relief against the nearly universal omission of similar subjects in the paint by number oeuvre.

While mass culture's critics believed education to be futile in remediating taste (considering education, like propaganda, to be necessary lubricants of a distended consumer society), by the Spring of 1954 art educators had adopted "numbers nonsense" as a professional rallying cry and point of attack. From *School Arts* magazine, D. Kenneth Winebrenner editorialized that "We can no longer ignore this threat to art education." Winebrenner wrote,

> We believe that this age of mechanical regimentation requires that everyone have some activity in which he may truly express himself creatively if we are not to have a sick culture. Painting by numbers, like ready-cut kits, prepared craft patterns, casting in manufactured molds, and other stereotyped products is stifling and inhibiting. In extending the standardizing influence of the machine to his leisure time activities the easily

Avalon First Prize. The promotion of paint by number as a meritorious activity traded upon this adaptation of an academic beaux arts sculpture medal.

deceived squelches his native urge for creative self-expression, and yields to the destructive powers that regiment and ruin the soul of man.[36]

Weinbrenner concluded that paint by number was "truly appalling," an "atrophying scheme," "a creative dead end," a "noncreative" art product that "tends to undermine the very philosophy of teaching." Educator Clyde C. Clack editorialized in the pages of *Art Educationist*, that the "old methods" had at least required "some effort at drawing and selecting one's own colors. The new 'road block' has eliminated all drawing and even the choosing or naming of colors, because the colors are numbered—also the spaces where they are to be placed—thus eliminating the need for all creative thinking."[37]

Although nearly all advertising—then as now—trades in the suspension of disbelief as a condition of its success, paint by number's critics suggested that its consumers actually believed the claims of "capsuled creativity" emblazoned on kit box tops.[38] One school teacher, for example, complained, "We see hundreds of people—even former pupils—rushing to the ten cent stores to buy these inane things.... How proudly they

proceed, as pleased with themselves as though they were actually doing something meritorious instead of meretricious. There ought to be a law!"[39] Another chronicler of the hobby's tendency to infuriate educators noted that real artists "hit the ceiling" at the mention of "numbers painting," citing Mrs. Lola Fitzgerald, an art instructor at North Chattanooga [Tennessee] Junior High School, who complained that paint by number stifled "the creative impulse in children." As for grown people, "If Grandma Moses had started out with a numbers kit, she'd never be where she is today."[40]

School Arts magazine, paint by number's most persistent educational critic, kept up its attack on "numbers nonsense" through 1955. Despite the publication of successive editorials warning school teachers and their administrators away from retrogressive "copycat" methods and "stultifying influences," the magazine's editors never fully articulated a plan of attack beyond denial.[41] The best that could be found was the "New Use for Number Sets" by Professor Howard S. Conant of the State College for Teachers at Buffalo. Conant and his daughter Judy salvaged paint pots and canvas boards for freehand compositions that otherwise dispensed with the system.[42]

LEFT: THERE OUGHTA BE A LAW. c. 1954. A Sunday cartoon lampooned the popularity of paint by number by representing it as an environmental condition, as did many period cartoons that ordered reality in the form of differentiated color blocks, in this case reminiscent of Palmer Paint's "personal portrait" kit.

RIGHT: Completing a child's "personal portrait" c. 1954. In 1954 Palmer Paint offered the "Personal Portrait" paint set. For twenty dollars, consumers received a specially created canvas board with the ready to paint outline of a portrait rendered from a photograph.

ABOVE: LIGHTHOUSE

OPPOSITE: YACHT RACE

Working outside the system, one hobbyist
elaborated on the composition by painting
the frames.

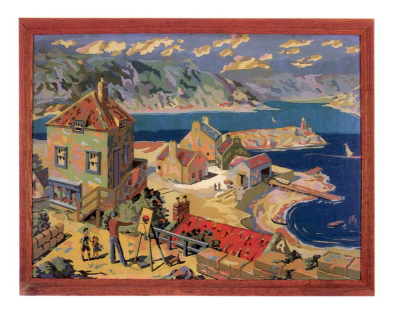

While art educators encouraged children to paint over the lines, as adult hobbyists gained confidence they too embellished their store-bought compositions. One painted out the waiting automobile in a snow scene. Another extended the sea and sky of a pair
of seascapes right out onto their frames. The hobby's most lasting effect similarly lay
beyond the finished composition in the mind of the consumer. Though paint by number
could not be recommended by educators charged with fostering the child's innate poten-
tial for creativity, as an adult matter the drumbeat of criticism suggesting that paint by
number hobbyists lacked the means with which to distinguish a work of art from the
work of art's incredible simulation was the era's lasting and unforgiving conceit.

TOP: WINTER SHADOWS. Adhering to every detail, a hobbyist completed this painting as intended.

BOTTOM: WINTER SHADOWS. Blurring the boundaries of art and craft, the hobbyist who completed this painting removed the waiting car, the fence along the right side of the road, and other details. Signed Susan Ellis.

CHAPTER THREE

THE PICTURE'S PLACE

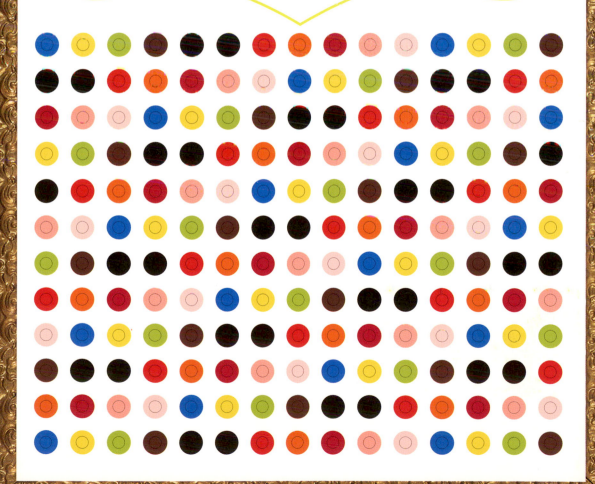

Shirley Rae Roll ÷ 1953

When it comes to accounts, the paint by number phenomenon was as much about who as what. The what was well-defined: color blocks, keyed palettes, and idle hours whiled away with *Suburb de Paris*, *Poppies in Composition*, and *Indian Summer*. The who was never as neatly circumscribed as the hobby's critics had it, for the picture's place, at home and in temporal experience, cut across fluid class lines. Many critics, for example, fit "number filler inners" to the template of the postwar suburban tract home, in which little culture was thought to exist, and none expected to grow. Though hobbyists of all classes and domiciles may have wished for different hobby choices, in its own modest way paint by number offered an outlet for craft, a sense of accomplishment, and a decorative step-up from the mounting of reproduction paintings and prints.

At home the picture's place called for careful thought and consideration. Like the advice dispensed in the pages of *Better Homes and Gardens*, *Good Housekeeping*, and

OPPOSITE:
FLORAL STILL
LIFE signed
Shirley Rae Roll,
1953

try these decorative ways to hang pictures

Probably the first rule of thumb in hanging pictures effectively is to keep them down at eye level where everyone can enjoy them. A picture over a mantel or sofa should be just three or four inches up, and should be of a size to command attention. Pictures should be used boldly and purposefully, whether hung singly or grouped. In creating a picture grouping above your fireplace or over the sofa, bear in mind that since they are focal spots of the room, they should have mass and importance. Here, more than anywhere else, watch for proper size balance.

When a single painting won't do the job, many decorators utilize several small pictures of assorted sizes, massed over the mantel, sofa, or a low bookshelf. In such a grouping, you can use a Craft Master painting and its accompanying pictures, both horizontal and vertical shapes, in a wide variety of subject matter. A good idea is to lay your pictures on the floor to decide what your hanging pattern will be before ever touching the wall. If you have painted pictures in matching pairs, you can display them two or four in the group. Perhaps two horizontals hung one above the other, flanked by two smaller verticals. Or an off-center arrangement, above a chest or sofa, could use a vertical painting, balanced by two small horizontals. Never feel that paintings have to be

hung dead center over any piece of furniture. They may be hung far left or far right and often make an interesting balance for lamps or flower arrangements.

As a general rule, avoid locations where the light is inadequate, or where the viewer is forced into an awkward position to see your work properly. Part of the pleasure of pictures is their ability to draw the eye to quickly give it a complete and pleasant impression. Don't feel that paintings

belong only in the living room. Many of today's smartest homes use them extensively in bedrooms, in entrance halls, in dining rooms or alcoves—in fact, every room in the house. Children who have painted Craft Master and Masterpiece canvases love to have a private "gallery" in their rooms. When hanging a group of small pictures of the same size, try framing them very simply, individually, and then hanging them inside a large empty frame. (See Page 51 for a large selection of frames that will complement your paintings.) Paintings which reflect someone's hobby—sailing, hunting, fishing, for example—may also be hung in a panel

treatment combined with things typical of the hobby. Try combining such symbols as barometers, lake charts, guns, rods, or samples of flies and lures to build a most interesting arrangement with your pictures. Whatever you decide to do with your paintings, do it with flare. Do it in such a way that your paintings speak out as important decorative accents. Used well, paintings can become a most effective factor in establishing the individuality and charm of your home.

"Try these decorative ways to hang pictures." Palmer Paint Company, 1954. Advice for first time framers.

Hobbies, kit pamphlets provided gentle guidance for first-time framers. The finished painting might be grouped with symbols and hobby materials such as "barometers, lake charts, guns, rods, or samples of flies and lures." The entire living quarters of the home was thought to deserve paintings, including the children's room, that might be turned into a "private 'gallery.'" Diagrams offered lessons in "picture grouping," "focal spots," "mass and importance," and "proper size balance." The literature warned against displaying paintings in inadequate light, "or where the viewer is forced into an awkward position to see your work properly." Palmer Paint urged, Whatever you decide to do with your paintings, do it with flare. Do it in such a way that your paintings speak out as important decorative accents. Used well, paintings can become a most effective factor in establishing the individuality and charm of your home.[1]

Fanciful trade literature idealized the personal place of the finished painting. A catalog for Testors' "Master Palette" line of "Paint by Letter" sets reiterated the point: "Day to day family relationships can be made more rewarding through pride in the home. Master Palette makes such beauty a possibility—easy [*sic*], economically, and elegantly."[2]

Detail, "Day-to-day
family relationships."
Testors

Period decorating magazines reported that because of the "millions" being spent on hobbies, homes were being enlarged, and space commandeered. "If hobbies are not putting a strain on the family budget," noted *House + Home*, "they are at least putting a strain on the space in which to do them." Basements in existing houses were transformed into hobby-workshop-recreation areas, and in new construction gave rise to the split level house.[3] While homemaking magazines described the quest for space, sociologists found hobbyists squeezed for quality creative time. In his study of Levittown's Willingboro, New Jersey (where as a matter of economy there were no basements), Herbert J. Gans observed that his neighbors had sacrificed creativity to the time-wrenching pressures of raising a family, running a household, and earning a living. For example, while the housewives with whom Gans had come in contact "had learned that creativity was desirable," now that they had become wives and mothers "the urge for creativity returned—but not the opportunity." Gans noted that they searched for "easy creativity, activities that do not require…'upsetting the family and household.'" Gans concluded that "serious artistic activity is difficult under such conditions, yet a compromise solution

LEFT:
FLORAL STILL
LIFE WITH
FIGURE

RIGHT:
FLORAL STILL
LIFE WITH
DEER FIGURE.
The vibrant pattern
of these frames
suggests a certain
acceptance of
abstract imagery in
home decor, con-
sistent with that
typically found in
Formica laminate
and floor tile.

such as needlework or painting-by-numbers is not entirely satisfactory, either, because, however rewarding, people know it is not really art." Gans' observation was stimulated by neighbors' reactions to his wife's hobby, abstract expressionist painting.[4]

Abstract paintings, as Dan Robbins and Max Klein learned, did not appeal to hobbyists drawn to paint by number. Sociological investigation in the late Fifties confirmed that lower-class home makers regarded abstract imagery with suspicion, with the possible exception of the patterns that embellished floor tile, Formica laminate, and picture frames. In choosing to frame subjects such as still lifes, landscapes, and seascapes, the paint by number hobbyist was not unique. Contemporary observers noted that the landscape predominated in most decorating schemes. Russell Lynes, for example, visited the picture buyer of Sears, Roebuck to learn what the customers of the world's largest retailer bought. The Sears buyer patiently explained that reproductions of the Masters—Rembrandt, Renoir, and Van Gogh—did not sell. Sears' best seller was "Fiery Peaks," described as "a picture of the Cascade Mountains either at sunset or sunrise, you can't tell which, and the sky is bright orange." Confirming the "general taste" of the con-

"DINNER IS ALL READY, HONEY. JUST HELP YOURSELF."
(Model-Helen Brush, Los Angeles Daily News)
(B. F. Beeman Co./Gene Alfred & Assoc.)

suming public with a visit to the picture department of a local department store, Lynes witnessed homemakers choosing pictures to match curtains and carpets. Lynes noted that the upper-class art collector "work[ed] the other way around, if at all," selecting furnishings that matched *his* pictures.[5]

The pursuit of decorative effects with paint by number did in fact pose domestic dilemmas at odds with the idealized displays pictured in homemaking magazines and hobby literature. Certain homemakers likened the process of paint by number to an obsession so absorbing that even the nominal standards of housekeeping were swept aside. The *Craft Master Scene*, for example, carried the testimonial of a Baltimore housewife. Characterized as a "Satisfied Dis-satisfied Customer," she wrote, "'I am sorry I ever saw any of your pictures. My home is disgraceful and I sit here all day and paint. I am also spending my husband's money which I ought to be saving. Please send me a list of any new subjects you have.'"[6] The *Los Angeles Daily News* enlarged upon this dilemma with a photograph of a smiling housewife painting at the dining table. Her husband's place setting consists of a fork, a plate, and on the plate a can opener. Playing

LEFT:
"Dinner is all ready . . . "

RIGHT:
HIBISCUS IN BLOOM

TOP LEFT: SNOW COVERED VILLAGE; **TOP CENTER:** SNOWSCAPE, BOY PULLING SLED. **TOP RIGHT:** SNOW-SCAPE WITH CHURCH; **MIDDLE LEFT:** ROCK, SURF AND SKY; **MIDDLE CENTER:** SWISS VILLAGE; **MIDDLE RIGHT:** AFTER THE SNOW, professionally framed; **BOTTOM LEFT:** FALL LANDSCAPE. **BOTTOM CEN-TER:** COVERED BRIDGE. A majority of Americans preferred landscapes for home decor.

CONFLICT
OF THE SEA

upon the do-it-yourself ethos of Fifties home life, the caption coyly suggests, "Dinner is all ready, Honey. Just help yourself." If paint by number contributed to liberation from gender responsibilities until the paint set, the limits of liberation could be read in the perfect compliment to the curtains, *Hibiscus in Bloom.*

The framing of the picture literally joined painting to craft.[7] Though the dimensions of paint by number canvases (and later canvas boards) fit widely available, standard-size frames, Palmer Paint extended the Craft Master franchise with a line of standard-size frame kits. Lovingly framed paintings occupied center stage, and even professional picture framers reported a booming business. The *Toledo Blade* reported the observation of a local picture framer who expressed surprise at the number of "big businessmen" who came to his shop with paint by number paintings to be framed. He noted, They're feeling like Rembrandt himself, and they pick and choose and compare frames. Maybe we've already framed six as exactly like it as peas in a pod, to each one it's his own original genuine masterpiece, and deserving of the best frame to be bought.[8]

A sampling of the paintings that turn up at today's flea markets, yard sales, and household goods auctions suggests that paint by number's marketers successfully read consumers' tastes. The overwhelming majority of paintings found today are in the frames in which their painters put them.

By the late Fifties the expression "by the numbers" had begun to displace "by the book" as a pejorative for formulaic products, predictive techniques, and ways of thinking that left little to chance. Ironically, the artistic direction of the hobby that inspired the pejorative for by-rote, artless performance, was determined not by focused market research, but by hobbyists who carried on an impassioned correspondence with its producers about painting subjects, in the hope of painting more. One grateful hobbyist who expressed such a hope described the process of watching the canvas "unfold" as "a joy to behold." Still other testimonials of revelatory effect confirmed that the picture's place lay in experience beyond the frame. As a woman exhibitor at the Stix, Baer & Fuller department store painting exhibition explained, "A tree used to be just a tree to me. Now I often see as many as ten different colors in a single tree."[9] Art itself aspired to no less.

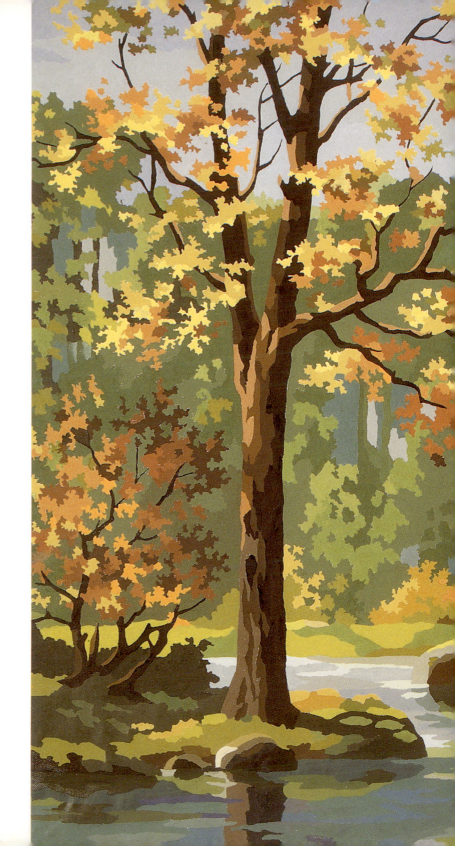

One of the largest
and most detailed
paint by number
subjects produced,
INDIAN SUMMER
featured a palette
of ninety colors, ten
of which may be
seen in the tree,
right foreground.

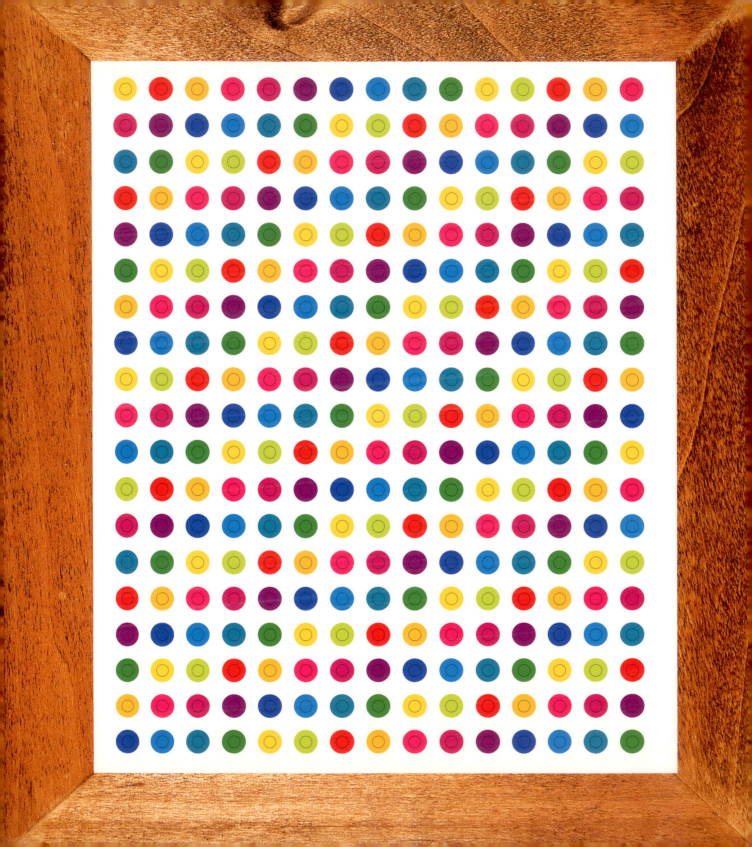

THE UNFINISHED WORK

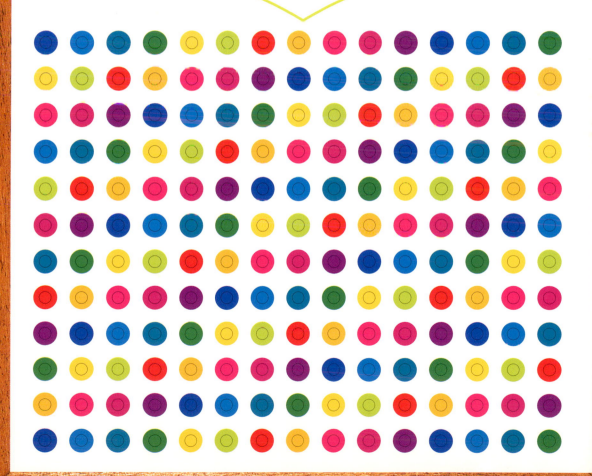

Before the close of the Fifties, paint by number was made

into a symbol of mass culture's corrosive influence upon taste. Its first use was concurrent with a loss of status among a cultural élite, at a time when democratic social values, prosperity, and a strong work ethic placed a premium upon leisure. Rooted in the memory of its popularity in that decade, paint by number has since become a metaphor for artless performance in American life and culture. In time, the consumption of mass culture as art—or not—receded as an index of social standing. This much could be seen in the appropriation of paint by number's outward form by the Pop Art movement of the early Sixties. In the political arena, the increasing use of social survey research to justify the institutional choices of the corporation and the state all but insured the continuing presence of paint by number as a metaphor for artless performance. Shortly thereafter, paint by number arrived as a popular pejorative for the mass market's predictive models and

effects, typically in the company of opinion sampling, motivational research, focus groups, and flow charts. By the early Nineties the paint by number phenomenon had come full circle as the paintings themselves became collectible.

Ironically, the company that did so much to make the world paint by number minded went into a financial tailspin at the height of the hobby's popularity. By late 1955 the bloom was off the phenomenon, at least for Max Klein and Palmer Paint (renamed the Palmer Pann Company that year). Thirty five competitors had entered the field, some of whom could and did match the quality of Dan Robbins and company's differentiated color block system. The rise of the mass discount house further undercut the return on Palmer's kits at the point of sale, squeezing profit margins on the markup of kits by the hobby and art supply dealers for whom paint by number had become a staple. While its low-priced kits flooded an already saturated market, Palmer Pann became overextended at the high end, committing personnel to Robbins' venture in "personal portraits." The labor-intensive process of creating portrait outlines—as many as three rendered from a single snapshot-could not be accomplished quickly enough to recover the cost of pro-

ducing a kit with which to render the most critically scrutinized consumer product imaginable, a painted portrait.[1] Tottering near bankruptcy, Klein sold his interest in Palmer Pann in late 1956, ending the firm's paint by number kit-making operations in Detroit. A line of do-it-yourself mosaic tile kits breathed life into Klein's next venture, but only momentarily.

Palmer Pann's new owners, Anthony D. Anton, Jr. and Anthony M.Donofrio, moved the kit-making operation from Detroit to Toledo, Ohio. Several artists followed, including Dick Hess, Peggy Grant, and Adam Grant. Within three years Toledo's Palmer Pann Company was described as the world's largest manufacturer of paint by number sets. The highly integrated operation rolled paint kits out of the company's Westwood Avenue plant at the rate of 20 tons a day. In 1963 Palmer Pann changed its name to Craft Master Corporation, reflecting its mainstay, the Craft Master paint set. The line remained a remarkably resilient commercial enterprise in an era of corporate diversification. When the company was sold to General Mills in 1967 for just under $6 million, annual sales were estimated at $9 million with a net after tax profit of $370,000.[2] While

LEFT:
Max Klein (left) and associates examining a mosaic table

RIGHT:
Jumbo Planter Boxes

OVERLEAF, LEFT AND RIGHT:
STILL LIFE

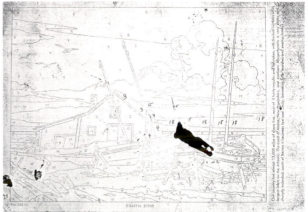

kits continued to be made for all age levels and incomes, the marketing of paint by number skewed toward entry level sets for adolescents and children, with a smattering of middle- to high-end sets for adults.

However dependent upon it, paint by number's most striking achievement lay outside the toy and hobby craft field in which it had become a staple. As the country entered a period of exuberant decor manifest in home furnishings and automotive styling characterized by the sweep of tail fins and the ornamental embellishment of refrigerators, vacuum cleaners, and television receivers,[3] consumers spent less time negotiating the undulating pattern of differentiated color blocks and keyed palettes. They were in fact spending more time with television, and therein lay the hobby's future as a metaphor for by-rote performance in television's Nielsen ratings age. As television became the primary focus of imaginary visual experience in the home, cultural critics, too, found new targets of enmity.[4]

Paint by number landscapes, seascapes and floral still life influenced the fine artist, through not in the way that the hobby's enthusiasts had once imagined it would. The

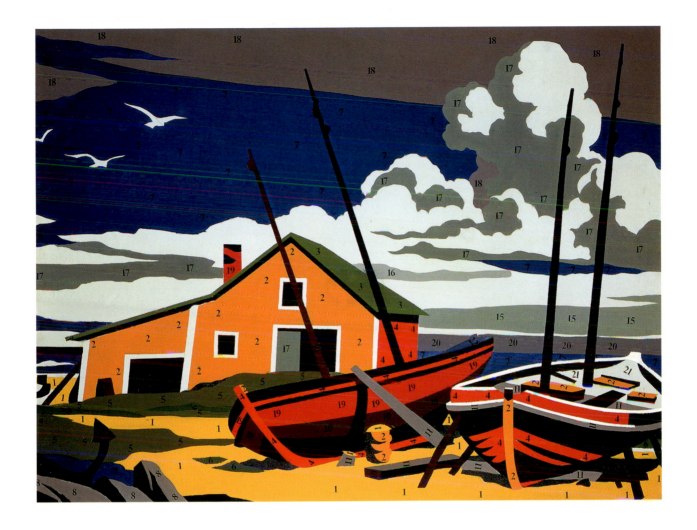

ABOVE: DO-IT-YOURSELF (SEASCAPE). Andy Warhol.
Synthetic polymer paint and Prestype on canvas. 1963. 54" x 6'.
Courtesy Heiner Bastian

OPPOSITE, LEFT: Venus Paradise 4 Pre-Sketched Drawings.
Commercial package for Venus Paradise pencil-by-number kit. Verso
used as a palette by Andy Warhol. No date, ca. early 1960s

OPPOSITE, RIGHT: COASTAL SCENE. Venus Pen & Pencil
Corporation. Source image for Warhol's painting DO IT YOURSELF
(SEASCAPE), 1963

TOP: DO·IT·YOURSELF (FLOWERS). Andy Warhol. 1962. Synthetic polymer paint and Prestype on canvas. 69 x 59". Courtesy The Daros Collection

BOTTOM LEFT: DO·IT·YOURSELF (NARCISSUS). Andy Warhol. 1962. Pencil and colored pencil on paper. 23 x 18". Courtesy Öffentliche Kunstsammlung Basel

BOTTOM RIGHT: DO IT YOURSELF (FLOWERS). 1962. Andy Warhol. Colored crayon on paper, 25 x 18". Lent by The Sonnabend Collection

OPPOSITE LEFT: DO·IT·YOURSELF (SAILBOATS). Andy Warhol. 1962. Acrylic paint and Prestype on canvas. 72 x 100". Courtesy The Daros Collection

OPPOSITE RIGHT: DO·IT·YOURSELF (LANDSCAPE). Andy Warhol. 1962. Synthetic polymer paint and Prestype on canvas. 70 x 54". Courtesy Museum Ludwig, Cologne

paintings became an especially rich vein of ready-to-mine source material for the Pop Art movement. The form's most celebrated appropriation was rendered by Andy Warhol, who painted a series of canvases entitled "Do It Yourself" during 1962-1963, the same period in which he painted serial canvases depicting the iconic Campbell's Soup can.

Often making photographs and advertising images the basis of his designs, Warhol used the outline images found in a Venus Paradise pencil-by-number drawing set for the "Do It Yourself" series. Warhol often complained that painting was "too hard." These examples of Warhol's most exquisite paintings began with the outline of a numbered picture. Warhol projected the image onto paper (for the purpose of study), and then to canvas, tracing the outline with the flat of his pencil. Warhol then painted the color blocks and applied Prestype numerals for decorative effect.[5]

Warhol's background as a commercial artist made his choice of subject material all the more notorious. The adjectives "mechanical" and "banal" were most often applied to the "Do It Yourself" series.[6] The reaction lingered for years. At the opening of a Warhol retrospective mounted by the Whitney Museum in the Seventies, a young assis-

ESQUIRE magazine cover art. Richard Hess. 1967. Courtesy of Samuel N. Antupit

tant who was unfamiliar with Warhol's career as a painter assumed that the exhibit's curator had made a mistake. Surely Warhol had not done that, the assistant wondered, pointing to a "Do It Yourself" canvas that Warhol had painted in 1962. Warhol later noted that his assistants' creative misinterpretation of assignments provided an open-ended supply of unanticipated effects, not unlike the "How did *that* get in here?" question that Warhol characteristically left unanswered. The "Do It Yourself" paintings were among the last paintings that Warhol made before turning to exclusively mechanical and infinitely reproducible means of production such as silk screen.[7]

The pervasive influence of the mass media and efforts to model and predict its ever-popular effects helped propel paint by number to the forefront of national political life in the latter half of the decade. Somehow escaping application to the policies and programs of the Eisenhower and Kennedy administrations, paint by number was metaphorically applied to the policies of President Lyndon Baines Johnson. A June 1967 *Esquire* magazine cover by former Palmer Paint staff artist Richard Hess portrayed the President as an unfinished-or incomplete-paint by number work. That year

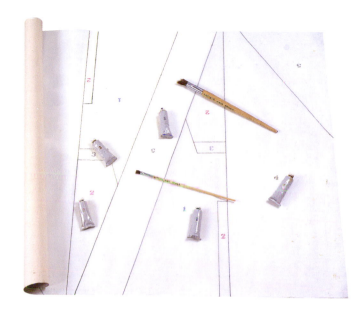

ABSTRACT PAINT BY
NUMBER KIT: AGAINST
THE LOOKING GLASS. Paul
Bridgewater. Unstretched
Canvas with accompanying typed
instruction sheet. 1978. 34 x
40 3/4". Lent by the Andy
Warhol Foundation

Johnson had had trouble finding an official portrait to his liking. Recognizing a feature when he saw it, *Esquire* art director Samuel N. Antupit commissioned leading artists and illustrators to mount Johnson's likeness on the Old Masters. Antupit commissioned Hess, who long after his work for Palmer Paint had become an illustrator of *Time* covers, to create a presidential portrait in the paint by number idiom. Hess' likeness of LBJ, however, was pulled at the last minute in deference to a preexisting agreement with the author of an article that required the cover spot, thus becoming the most famous *Esquire* cover that never ran. The cover layout later won numerous awards and medals; was included in exhibitions at the Art Directors Club, the American Institute of Graphic Arts, and the Society of Illustrators; and was reproduced in *Print* magazine and various catalogs including the *Art Director's Annual*, winning awards for Hess and Antupit. It was also exhibited in a show at the Louvre.[8]

In 1987 artist Paul Bridgewater created five abstract paint by number kits that sold to Andy Warhol and Fernando Botero. The kit idea came to Bridgewater during a tour of the Los Angeles County Museum of Art, in which the docent giving the tour dismissed the museum's collection of contemporary art as "simplistic." Drawing upon childhood memory, Bridgewater set out to make "a great work of art that even a seven year old could do." Bridgewater later recalled being given paint by number subjects to paint by his mother, who favored paint by number landscapes, especially covered bridges.[9] In 1992 the artist's Bridgewater/Lustberg Gallery exhibited the paint by number collection of screenwriter Michael O'Donoghue, whose articulate defense of the hobby inspired a resurgent interest in collecting and exhibiting the paintings.[10]

In 1993 Vitaly Komar and Alex Melamid won a $40,000 grant from the Nation Foundation for the purpose of making a telephone survey of Americans' tastes in art. The Russian émigrés, who lived and worked in Bayonne, New Jersey, conceived the survey as a continuation of their work "to get in touch with the people of the United States of America, somehow to penetrate their brains, to understand their wishes—to be a real part of this society of which we're partially part, partially not." Komar and Melamid interpreted survey results in the paintings *America's Most Wanted* (dishwasher size) and *America's Least Wanted* (paperback size). The results were oddly familiar to anyone who has ever contemplated paint by number. Survey respondents expressed an overwhelming preference for landscapes. Forty per cent preferred the color blue, that found its way into a cloudless sky above a mountain lake. Preferences for other elements were rendered proportionately—a tourist family, frolicking deer, and a figure of George Washington. Critical reaction to the paintings was almost as predictable. Comments posted on a website set up to poll the World Wide Web's most and least wanted paintings ran the gamut from enthusiasm to incredulity. One survey respondent complained, "It looks made by the manager of a third rate supermarket trying to understand the taste of his suburban customers." To which the artists replied, "American grocery stores are the best grocery stores in the world, which you can't say about American art." Critics applauded the project's attempt to establish a dialogue with art's audience, or at least, the appearance of one.[11] In our current political climate, paint by number may be the perfect metaphor for the mechanization and commercialization of culture in which even the élite art consumer has become a demographic unit of measurement among competitive taste publics.

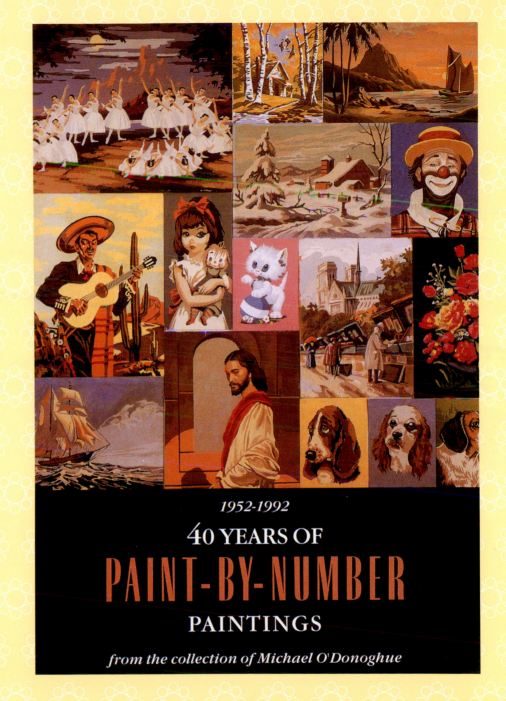

1952-1992

40 YEARS OF

PAINT-BY-NUMBER

PAINTINGS

from the collection of Michael O'Donoghue

Exhibition postcard, Bridgewater/
Lustberg Gallery

ABOVE: AMERICA'S MOST WANTED. Vitaly Komar and Alex Melamid. 1994. Acrylic on canvas. Dishwasher size. Courtesy of Vitaly Komar and Alex Melamid

OPPOSITE, LEFT: AMERICA'S LEAST WANTED. Vitaly Komar and Alex Melamid. 1994. Acrylic on canvas. Paperback size. Courtesy of Vitaly Komar and Alex Melamid

OPPOSITE, RIGHT: PEOPLE'S CHOICE COLOR PREFERENCES. Vitaly Komar and Alex Melamid. 1994. Acrylic on canvas. 48 x 60". Courtesy of Vitaly Komar and Alex Melamid

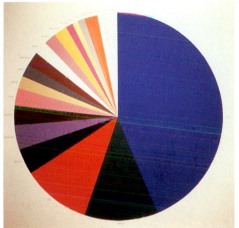

Once the vessel for anxieties about mass culture's intrusion into the well-upholstered world of taste and social class, paint by number reflected the democratization of culture in a time of anxiety and uncertainty about the quantity and quality of life. Paint by number confounded the harshest of critics, who persisted with the "they don't know what they are doing" line of attack long after the hobby's heyday. Yet the satisfaction found in crafts and hobbies that critics were first to recognize had become central to, as Palmer Paint's box tops would have it, "the art of creative relaxation." Having it all, paint by number's willing consumers blurred the postwar era's boundaries of social expectation. Paint by number's subsequent adoption as a metaphor spoke volumes about the crisis of culture set off by the problem of leisure, whose solution visited and revisited the open questions of taste, class, and worth. By those standards the picture's place in national life and culture became secure, never more so than today, ever decorative, ironic, and scandalously artistic.

Introduction

1 "These Fads Have Built a Billion Dollar Business," *Business Week* (November 28, 1953): 78–86; "Paint by Numbers Fad Sweeping the Nation," *The Register*, Santa Ana, CA, 3 May 1953: sec. B7.

2 Leo Lowenthal, "Historical Perspectives of Popular Culture," in Bernard Rosenberg and David Manning White,eds., *Mass Culture: The Popular Arts in America* (New York: The Free Press, 1957): 55, cited in Herbert J. Gans, *Popular Culture and High Culture: An Analysis and Evaluation of Taste* (New York: Basic Books, 1974): 20.

3 Frances E. and Fred Burry to Kevin Kolde, September 22, 1994, Dan Robbins collection, copy in the possession of the author. Dan Robbins notes that a patent search initiated by the Palmer Paint Company in the period 1949–1950 turned up "multiple numbers of the 'by-the-numbers' concepts" including several paint by number patent filings dating to 1923. Robbins, *Whatever Happened to Paint-by-Numbers?* (Delavan, WI: Possum Hill Press, 1997): 23–24.

4 In contrast to the author's personal experience, "sad" is the term that contemporary critics most frequently employed to describe suburban life. Randall Jarrell, "A Sad Heart at the Supermarket," in Norman Jacobs,ed., *Culture for the Millions? Mass Media in Modern Society* (Princeton, NJ: D. Van Nostrand Company Inc., 1959 and 1961): 97–110; David Riesman, "The Suburban Sadness," in William Dobriner, ed., *The Suburban Community* (New York: G. B. Putnam's Sons, 1958): 375–408; John Keats, *The Crack in the Picture Window* (New York: Ballantine Books, 1956): *passim*.

5 Lawrence W. Levine, *Highbrow/Lowbrow: The Emergence of Cultural Hierarchy in America* (Cambridge: Harvard University Press, 1988): 161–163.

6 Reader J. L. K., cited in Arthur L. Guptill, "Amateur Page," *American Artist* 17 (December 1953): 58.

7 Reader R. R. S., cited in Arthur L. Guptill, "Amateur Page," *American Artist* 17 (December 1953): 58–59.

8 Gans, *Popular Culture and High Culture: An Analysis and Evaluation of Taste*; Levine, *Highbrow/Lowbrow*; Lears, "A Matter of Taste;" Michael Kammen, *American Culture, American Tastes: Social Change and the 20th Century* (New York: Alfred K. Knopf, 1999), especially chapter 5, "Blurring the Boundaries Between Taste Levels": 95–132; Karal Ann Marling, *As Seen on TV: The Visual Culture of Everyday Life in the 1950s* (Cambridge: Harvard University Press, 1994): 50–84; Marling. "From the Quilt to the Neocolonial Photograph: The Arts of the Home in an Age of Transition," in Jessica H. Foy and Marling, eds., *The Arts and the American Home, 1890–1930.* (Knoxville: University of Tennessee Press, 1994): 1–13, esp. 5–6.

9 David A Karns and Steven J. Smith, "Visitor Familiarity with Paint by Number" (typescript), Institutional Studies Office, Smithsonian Institution, March 2000.

Chapter One

1 Herb Caen, "Baghdad by the Bay," *San Francisco Examiner*, 20 October 1952: 29, cited in Robbins, *Whatever Happened to Paint by Numbers?*: 176. Caen's column followed by a little over a month a feature story about the new hobby. "Painting by the Numbers." *San Francisco Chronicle*, 7 September 1952: 1, sec. 9L.

2 "Art by the Numbers," *Time* 61 (May 4, 1953): 94–96.

3 Lois M. Luntz, "Personalities and publicity put Palmer in first place." *The Hobby Merchandiser* (September 1953): 32–35.

4 Robbins, *Whatever Happened to Paint by Numbers?*: 14–17.

5 David Deitcher, "Unsentimental Education: The Professionalization of the American Artist," in Russell Ferguson, ed. *Hand-Painted Pop: American Art in Transition, 1952–1962.* Exhibition catalog, (Los Angeles: Museum of Contemporary Art, 1992): 95–118.

6 Robbins, *Whatever Happened to Paint by Numbers?*: 16–23.

7 Defining the audience for abstract and representational or narrative art has been the preoccupation of postwar critics' construction of taste and its equivalent, class. For example, Herbert J. Gans, turning his attention to the "taste public" of lower middle-class art in the early Seventies, found this group more willing to buy art than in the past. Its art shunned abstraction, paid less attention to "creators" than to subject matter, though allowances were made for "imitations" of cubist forms ("altered in a more representational direction") and "the landscapes of Cezanne and Van Gogh, the dancers of Degas, and the cityscapes of Buffet." Gans, *Popular Culture and High Culture*: 87–88.

8 Robbins, *Whatever Happened to Paint by Numbers?*: 78–79

9 Louise Bruner, "The Figure Paintings of Adam Grant," *American Artist* 37 (January 1973): 24–27, 71; "Through Craft Master Kits Award-Winning 'Sunday Artist' Guides Brushes of Thousands," 10–11, clipping in possession of Peggy Grant; Sally Vollongo, "Taking Art to the Source," *Toledo Blade*, 28 January 1998: 30, 33; Kim Edwards, "Telling it on the Mountain: Peggy Grant's quest to keep her husband's legacy alive," *Toledo City Paper* (August 1999): 46; Robbins, *Whatever Happened to Paint by Numbers?*: 88–92, 113–123.

10 "We Paint a Picture" [n.d.], box 9 f 1, Paint by Number Collection, Archives Center, National Museum of American History (hereafter PBN/NMAH).

11 "Industry Expands to Meet Demand," *The Craft Master Scene* 1, no. 4 (September 1953), PBN/NMAH.

12 Luntz, "Personalities and publicity put Palmer in first place": 32–35.

13 "Coronation Theme in New CM Set," *Craft Master Scene* 1 (July 1953): 4.

14 Dan Robbins, interview with the author, December 15, 1999, Evanston, IL. For contemporary discussion of the making of a "fad," see Rolf Meyersohn and Elihu Katz, "Notes on a Natural History of Fads," in Eric Larrabee and Rolf Meyersohn, eds., *Mass Leisure* (New York: The Free Press, 1958): 305–315.

15 "These Fads Have Built a Billion-Dollar Business," *Business Week* (November 28, 1953): 78–86; Marling, *As Seen on TV*, 63.

Chapter Two

1 Bendiner concluded, "Right now it is business that is selling the life of leisure, and the life of leisure that business can sell is necessarily a life of Aqua lungs, outboard motors, Scotch Koolers and house paint—all good in their way, no doubt, but none of them suggesting for a moment that there was more to Greece than marathons and more to Rome than baths." Robert Bendiner, "Could You Stand a Four-Day Week?" *The Reporter* 17 (August 8, 1957): 10–14.

2 "The Leisured Masses," *Business Week* (September 12, 1953): 142–152.

3 E. E. Calkins, "The New Leisure: A Curse or a Blessing?" *Economic Forum* 1 (Fall 1933): 371–382; M. C. Winston, "The New Leisure," *Progressive Education* 4 (October – December 1927): 315–317; Stuart Chase, "Leisure in a Machine Age," *Library Journal* 56 (August 1931): 629–632; P. L. Benjamin, "The New Leisure," *Recreation* 29 (July 1935): 187–189, 222–223; E. Lyons, "Menace of Leisure," *American Mercury* 48 (December 1939): 477–479; William Graebner, *The Engineering of Consent: Democracy and Authority in Twentieth-Century America* (Madison: University of Wisconsin Press, 1987): 3–6, *passim*.

4 David Riesman, "Leisure and Work in Post-Industrial Society," in Eric Larrabee and Rolf Meyersohn, eds., *Mass Leisure*: 363–385. Looking back over the decade, sociologist Daniel Bell reached a similar conclusion. Chronicling the "fantastic mushrooming" of period "arts-and-crafts hobbies, of photography, home woodwork shops with power-driven tools, ceramics, high-fidelity, electronics, radio 'hams,'" Bell noted that "America has seen the multiplication of the 'amateur' on a scale unknown in previous history. And while this is intrinsically commendable, it has been achieved at a high cost indeed—the loss of satisfaction in work." Daniel Bell, *The End of Ideology: On the Exhaustion of Political Ideas in the Fifties* (Cambridge: Harvard University Press, 1960): 259.

5 Steven M. Gelber, *Hobbies: Leisure and the Culture of Work in America* (New York: Columbia University Press, 1999): 15–20, 268–294; Carolyn M. Goldstein, *Do It Yourself: Home Improvement in 20th Century America*, (New York: Princeton Architectural Press, 1998); Albert Roland,"Do-It-Yourself: A Walden for the Millions?" *American Quarterly* 10 (Summer 1958): 154–164; Marling, *As Seen on TV*: 50–84.

6 "How Do YOU Rate in the New Leisure? Russell Lynes, A Witty Observer, Charts a New Class System." *Life* 47 (December 28, 1959): 85–89. A similar feature ten years earlier described "three basic categories of a new U. S. social structure," in which "the high-brows have the whip hand." "High-Brow, Low-Brow, Middle-Brow," *Life* 26 (April 11, 1949): 99–102, pictured in Michael Kammen, *American Culture, American Tastes: Social Change in the 20th Century* (New York: Alfred A. Knopf, 1999): 97–99.

7 William C. DeVane, quoted in Reuel Denney and David Riesman, "Leisure and Human Values in Industrial Civilization," in Eugene Staley, ed., *Creating an Industrial Civilization* (New York: Harper & Bros., 1952): 50–91, quoted 74; Denney, "Leisure in Industrial America," in Staley, ed., *Creating an Industrial Civilization*, 245–281; Bendiner, "Could You Stand a Four-Day Week?"

8 Harvey Swados, "Less Work, Less Leisure," in Larrabee and Meyersohn, *Mass Leisure*: 353–363.

9 Margaret Mead, "The Pattern of Leisure in Contemporary American Culture," *Annals of the American Academy of Political and Social Science* 313 (September 1957): 11–15; Mead's essay may also be found in Larrabee and Meyersohn, *Mass Leisure*: 10–14.

10 Lewis Mumford, *The City in History* (New York: Harcourt, Brace, 1961): 486, cited in Clifford E. Clark, Jr., "Ranch-House Suburbia: Ideals and Realities," in Lary May, ed., *Recasting America: Culture and Politics in the Age of Cold War* (Chicago: University of Chicago Press, 1989): 171–191.

11 William H. Whyte, *The Organization Man* (New York: Simon and Schuster, 1956): 310, cited in Lears, "A Matter of Taste: Corporate Cultural Hegemony in a Mass-Consumption Society," in Lary May, *Recasting America*: 38–57.

12 For a critical assessment of art and consumer culture that anticipated the arrival of paint by number see Clement Greenberg, "The Present Prospects of American Painting and Sculpture," (1947), in John O'Brian, ed., *The Collected Essays and Criticism, Vol. 2: Arrogant Purpose 1945–1949* (Chicago: University of Chicago Press, 1986): 160–170; Deitcher, "Unsentimental Education; In a 1949 article that later appeared as a chapter in *The Tastemakers: The Shaping of American Popular Taste* (New York: 1954). Russell Lynes characterized "highbrow" disdain for consumerism's well advertised excesses, "the dead weight around the neck of progress, the gag in the mouth of art." Lynes, "Highbrow, Lowbrow, Middlebrow." *Harper's* 198 (February 1949): 19–28; *The Tastemakers*, 332.

13 "Movie Theatre Plan is Given," *The Craft Master Scene* 1 (April 1953): 4.

14 On the subject of craft, David Riesman noted that "There is a widespread trend today to warn Americans against relaxing in the featherbed of plenty, in the pulpy recreations of popular culture . . . In these warnings any leisure that looks easy is suspect, and craftsmanship does not look easy." Riesman, *The Lonely Crowd* (New Haven: Yale University Press, 1950), 333–336, cited in Alfred C. Clarke, "Leisure and Occupational Prestige," in Eric Larrabee and Rolf Meyersohn, eds., *Mass Leisure*: 205–214, quote, 210–211.

15 "Painting Contests Excellent Publicity," *Craft Master Scene* (May 1953): 3.

16 "Business Boom for Young Promotion-Minded Firm," *Art Materials Trade News* x (January 1954): 25, 36.

17 Eric Larrabee, "What's Happening to Hobbies?" in Larrabee and Meyersohn, *Mass Leisure*: 268–274.

18 Joe Shannon to the author (typescript), n.d.

19 Transcript, respondent #252, Karns and Smith, "Visitor Familiarity with Paint by Number."

20 Transcript, respondent #317, Karns and Smith, "Visitor Familiarity with Paint by Number."

21 Clifford T. Rogers, "New Art Comes of Age 'By-the-Numbers'" (reprint), *The Craft Master Scene* 1 no. 5 (December 1953): 2, NMAH.

22 Peter C. Marzio, *The Art Crusade: An Analysis of American Drawing Manuals, 1820–1860* (Washington, D.C.: Smithsonian Institution Press, 1976): 18–23, 45–53.

23 Leonard Brooks, "You Too Can Paint," *Atlantic Monthly* 195 (June 1955): 86.

24 Lynn Spigel, *Make Room for TV: Television and the Family Ideal in Postwar America* (Chicago: University of Chicago Press, 1992): 17; Albert Roland, "Do-It-Yourself: A Walden for the Millions?": 154–164.

25 Lawrence W. Levine notes that the nineteenth century's cultural critics charged that the mechanical means of reproduction and diffusion contributed to art's dilution. Though "gratifying" to the senses, critics deemed such objects to be inauthentic, machine-made interventions between "the creator and the product . . . not to be accorded artistic status." Levine, *Highbrow/Lowbrow*: 161–164; Peter Marzio, "A Chromo Civilization," *Mr. Audobon and Mr. Bein: Early Phase in the History of American Chromolithography* (Washington, D.C.: Smithsonian Institution, 1975): 1–2.

26 Bernard De Voto, "Why Professors Are Suspicious of Business," *Fortune* 43 (April 1951): 114–115, 139, 140, 142, 144.

27 Clement Greenberg, "Avant Garde and Kitsch," *Partisan Review* 6 (Fall 1939): 34–49; also in Greenberg, ed., *The Collected Essays and Criticism* Vol. 1, *Perceptions and Judgments 1939–1944* (Chicago: University of Chicago Press, 1986): 5–22. In the early Fifties Greenberg described the "sweetening" and "simplifying" of art for the middle class market as a greater threat to high art than Kitsch itself. Clement Greenberg, "Review of the Water-Color, Drawing, and Sculpture Sections of the Whitney Annual," 1946, in John O'Brian, ed., *The Collected Essays and Criticism* Vol. 2, *Arrogant Purpose 1945–1949* (Chicago: University of Chicago Press, 1986): 57–59, cited in Deitcher, "Unsentimental Education." Appropriately enough the most succinct statement of the idea within is found on the dust jacket of Gillo Dorfles, *Kitsch: The World of Bad Taste.* (New York: Bell Publishing Company, 1975).

28 Janet K. Smith, "Art and the Homemaker," *Journal of Home Economics* 41 (November 1949): 497–498.

29 "Paint by Numbers Fad Sweeping Nation; $80,000,000 Worth Sold." Han van Meegeren was a notorious forger of works attributed to Vermeer. During the German occupation of Holland during the Second World War, van Meegeren had sold a "Vermeer" to Field Marshall Goering. Arrested after the war as a Nazi collaborator for his association with Goering, van Meegeren revealed the hoax to a disbelieving court. He mounted a successful self-defense by painting another "Vermeer." Russell Lynes, *The Tastemakers*: 278–279.

30 Karns and Smith, "Visitor Familiarity with Paint By Number."

31 Dwight D. Eisenhower, *At Ease: Stories I Tell to Friends* (New York: Doubleday & Co., 1967): 340–341; Mary Caffrey Stephens, telephone interview with the author, June 16, 2000.

32 Betty Beale, "Cabinet Painters Take Chief's Cue," *Washington Star*, 6 February 1955: sec.D, 1; Ruth Montgomery, "D.C. Wash," New York *Daily News* 4 March 1955; William Knighton, Jr., "That's Washington," Baltimore *Sun*, 14 October 1956: 19.

33 Cary Reich, *The Life of Nelson A. Rockefeller: Worlds to Conquer, 1908–1996* (New York: Doubleday, 1996): 65–67; Joseph E. Persico, *The Imperial Rockefeller: A Biography of Nelson A. Rockefeller* (New York: Simon and Schuster, 1982), 174–182, 289–290; *The Nelson Rockefeller Collection* (New York: Nelson Rockefeller Collection, Inc. 1978).

34 Sylvia Jukes Morris, *Rage for Fame: The Ascent of Clare Boothe Luce* (New York: Random House, 1997): 26, 38.

35 Todd Gitlin, *The Sixties: Years of Hope, Days of Rage* (New York: Bantam Books, 1987):16; Michael O'Donoghue, "A Head for Numbers," *House & Garden* 164 (November 1992): 74–76; Marling, *As Seen on TV*, 64.

36 Kenneth D. Winebrenner, "Numbers Nonsense," *The School Arts Magazine* 53 (January 1954): 4; "Creative Citizens," *The School Arts Magazine* 54 (May 1955): 48.

37 "Shell Your Own Corn." *Recreation* 47 (February 1954): 72.

38 David Manzella, "Numbered Paintings, Player Pianos, and Love Potions," *The School Arts Magazine* 55 (June 1956): 24–26.

39 On advertising see Leo Spitzer, *A Method of Interpreting Literature* (Northampton, MA: Smith College, 1949; reprint ed., New York: Russell and Russell, 1967); art teacher A. G. M., cited in Arthur L. Guptill, "Amateur Page," *American Artist* 17 (December 1953): 58–59.

40 Mary M'Donald Reynolds, "It's by the Numbers," *Chattanooga Times*, 16 May 1954.

41 Winebrenner, "Numbers Nonsense," *The School Arts Magazine* 53 (January 1954): 4; "Let Them Make Mistakes," *The School Arts Magazine* 53 (March 1954): 48; "Process or Product," *The School Arts Magazine* 53 (June 1954): 48; "Creative Citizens," *The School Arts Magazine* 54 (May 1955): 48; "What Makes It Art?" *The School Arts Magazine* 55 (December 1955): 48.

42 "New Use for Number Sets." *The School Arts Magazine* 54 (March 1955): 29.

Chapter Three

1 Trade catalog, *Paint a beautiful picture the first time you try with Craft Master* (Detroit: Palmer Paint Company, 1954): 54–55. This catalog was included with every Craft Master paint set from 1954 through 1955. For comparable advice, see Florence Byerly, "See What You Can Do With Pictures!" *Better Homes and Gardens* 33 (June 1955): 84–85; "Decorate to Enjoy Your Hobby More," *Better Homes and Gardens* 31 (October 1953): 214; "Dramatize Your Walls," *Good Housekeeping* 139 (September 1954): 181B; "Little Picture Galleries," *Good Housekeeping* 139 (October 1954): 196; "A.B.C's of Print and Picture Collecting," *Hobbies* 55 (November 1952): 46–47.

2 Trade catalog, *Fun for the Entire Family* (Rockford, IL: The Testor Corporation, c. 1962), collection of Larry Rubin.

3 "Room to Enjoy the New Leisure," *House and Home* 5 (May 1954): 134–137.

4 Herbert J. Gans, *The Levittowners: Ways of Life and Politics in a New Suburban Community* (New York: Columbia University Press, 1982): 203–204.

5 Lynes, *The Tastemakers*: 282–283. In his recent study of art's use in the American home, sociologist David Halle notes the popularity of landscapes across class lines. The nearly universal preference for landscapes, Halle suggests, parallels "the taste for suburbanization, and, indeed, amounts now almost to an obsession." Halle, *Inside Culture: Art and Class in the American Home* (Chicago: University of Chicago Press, 1993): 68. See also, Michael Kimmelman, "Painting by Numbers: How Bad Was It?" *New York Times*, 9 October 1994: sec. 2, 34.

6 Marling, *As Seen on TV*: 62.

7 Albert Roland noted that observers of the do-it-yourself movement treated painting no differently than crafts. "The practical utility of handicrafts has been almost entirely destroyed by the machine, but the avocational and recreational significance of these activities remains and is perhaps destined to increase," because craft emphasized the "importance of the physical thing." "For people involved in today's huge, anonymous processes of production and distribution," a 1954 *Time* cover story on do-it-

yourself said, "'it is hard to see what they are really accomplishing..'" Roland, "Do-It-Yourself: A Walden for the Millions?":154–164.

8 Aline Jean Treanor, "Know Numbers? Then Paint a Masterpiece," *Toledo Blade* 22 March 1953: sec. 5, 1.

9 "Store's Art Display Draws Large Crowd," *The Craft Master Scene* 1 no. 6 (February 1954): 3.

Epilogue

1 Robbins, *Whatever Happened to Paint-By-Numbers?*: 109–110; 128–140; 186–189.

2 Robbins notes that Anton and Donofrio, whose company supplied Palmer Pann with pre-packaged paints, purchased the company from Klein, their major contractor, in "self defense." Robbins, *Whatever Happened to Paint-By-Numbers?*: 192–193. On the subsequent history of Palmer Pann and its corporate successors, see Bernard Judy, "Toledo Firm Cashing In On Growth of Paint-By-Numbers Hobby," *Toledo Blade* 26 October 1958; "Palmer-Pann Changes Name," *Toledo Blade*, 21 October 1963; "Toledo Firm Bought By General Mills," *Toledo Blade* 6 September 1967; Homer Brickey, "Hobby Firm Eying Bigger Picture," *Toledo Blade* 18 April 1971; Bruce Vernyi, "Toledo: the Paint By-Numbers Capital?" *Toledo Blade*, 26 August 1984. On the Craft Master line's subsequent history with General Mills' Fun Dimensions division, Kenner Parker Toy, Craft House, Inc., RPM Corporation, and Brynwood Partners LLP, see Brickey, "Craft House Corp. Adds Products, Firms To Its Marketing Strategy," *Toledo Blade*, 19 September 1986; Brickey, "Toledo's Craft House helps boost parent into Fortune 500," *Toledo Blade*, 8 April 1994; Ben Klayman, "Craft House sale made," *Toledo Blade* 14 June 1997.

3 Shelley K. Nickles, "Object Lessons: Household Appliance Design and the American Middle Class, 1920–1960," Ph.D. dissertation, University of Virginia, 1999, esp. chapter 5.

4 Ian Brown, "Take a Number" *Globe and Mail* [Toronto, CN], 24 July 1999: sec. C: 1, 5.

5 Patrick S. Smith, *Warhol: Conversations About the Artist* (Ann Arbor, MI: UMI Research Press, 1988): 60, 64–65, 164–165.

6 John Coplans, for example, describing Warhol's impersonal style, wondered, "Can a painting be made that looks mechanical but is not?" Warhol had transformed "these banal images" into "strange paintings that are themselves supremely banal metaphors for paintings." John Coplans, "Early Warhol: The Systematic Evolution of the Impersonal Style," *Artforum* 8 (March 1970): 52–59; "Man for the Machine," *Time* 212 (May 24, 1971): 68–69; Ronald Tavel, "Theatre of the Ridiculous," *Tri-Quarterly* 6 (Spring 1966): 92–109.

7 Andy Warhol, *The Philosophy of Andy Warhol: From A to B and Back Again* (New York: Harcourt Brace and Company, 1975), 99; Warhol and Pat Hackett, *POPism: The Andy Warhol '60s* (New York: Harcourt Brace and Company, 1980): 182; Smith, *Warhol: Conversations About the Artist*: 204–205; Benjamin H. D. Buchloh, "Andy Warhol's One-Dimensional Art: 1956–1966," and Marco Livingstone,"Do It Yourself: Notes on Warhol's Techniques," in Kynaston McShine (ed.), *Andy Warhol: A Retrospective* (New York: Museum of Modern Art, 1989): 39–61, 63–78.

8 The original painting cannot be located, despite several attempts by Antupit to do so in the late Seventies. Samuel N. Antupit to author, September 17, 1999.

9 Paul Bridgewater, telephone interview with the author, July 22, 2000; Robbins, *Whatever Happened to Paint-by-Numbers?*, 261.

10 Michael O'Donoghue, "A Head for Numbers," *House & Garden* 164 (November 1992): 74–76.

11 Andrew Ross, "Poll Stars," *ArtForum* (January 1995): 72–77, 109; "Painting by Numbers: The Search for a 'People's Art.'" *The Nation* (March 14, 1994): 334–348; website quoted, http://www.dia-center.org/km/letters.html; JoAnn Wypijewski (ed.), *Painting By Numbers: Komar and Melamid's Scientific Guide to Art* (New York: Farrar, Straus & Giroux, 1997).

"A.B.C's of Print and Picture Collecting." *Hobbies* 55 (November 1952): 46–7.

Adkins, F. J. "The New Leisure." *Industrial Welfare* 16 (October 1934): 42–43.

Allport, Floyd H. "This Coming Era of Leisure." *Harper's* 163 (November 1931): 641–652.

"The Amateur Art Menace: An Editorial." *American Artist* 17 (May 1953): 3.

"Amateur Painting: It's A 'Craze.'" *Newsweek* 43 (January 11, 1954): 50–52.

America and the Intellectuals: A Symposium. New York: Partisan Review Press, 1953.

"Anderson, Harold H. "The Good Use of Leisure Time: Self-Expression Through Creativity." In W. Donahue, W. W. Hunter, D. H. Coons, and H .K. Maurice, eds. *Free Time: Challenge to Later Maturity.* Ann Arbor, MI: University of Michigan Press, 1958, pp.141–149.

"Art and the Leisure Time of Workers." *Monthly Labor Review* 41 (November 1935): 1235–1240.

"Art by the Numbers." *Time* 61 (May 4, 1953): 94–96.

Beale, Betty. "Cabinet Painters Take Chief's Cue." *Washington Star* 6 February 1955: sec. D, 1.

Beck, Edward J. "Painting by Number, Current National Craze, Started in Detroit." *Detroit News Pictorial Magazine,* 29 March 1953: 9.

Becker, Howard. *Art Worlds.* Berkeley, CA: University of California Press, 1982.

Belgrad, Daniel. *The Culture of Spontaneity: Improvisation and the Arts in Postwar America.* Chicago: University of Chicago Press, 1998.

Bell, Daniel. *The End of Ideology: On the Exhaustion of Political Ideas in the Fifties.* New York: Free Press, 1962, and Cambridge, MA: Harvard University Press, 1988.

Bendiner, Robert. "Could You Stand a Four-Day Week?" *Reporter* 17 (August 8, 1957): 10–14.

Benjamin, P. L. "The New Leisure." *Recreation* 29 (July 1935): 187–189, 222–223.

Benjamin, Walter. "The Work of Art in the Age of Mechanical Reproduction." In Walter Benjamin, *Illuminations.* New York: Schocken, 1968, pp. 219–253.

Berger, Bennett M. "Suburbia and the American Dream." *The Public Interest* (Winter 1966): 80–92.

Berger, Bennett M. *Working Class Suburb.* Berkeley and Los Angeles: University of California Press, 1960.

Bode, Carl. *The Anatomy of American Popular Culture, 1840–1860.* Berkeley and Los Angeles: University of California Press, 1960.

Bogart, Michele H. *Advertising, Artists, and the Borders of Art.* Chicago: University of Chicago Press, 1995.

Bourdieu, Pierre. *Distinction: A Social Critique of the Judgment of Taste.* Cambridge: Harvard University Press, 1984.

Bourdon, David. *Warhol.* New York: Abradale Press / Harry R. Abrams, 1989.

Brickey, Homer. "Craft House Corp. Adds Products, Firms To Its Marketing Strategy." *Toledo Blade,* 19 September 1986.

———. "Hobby Firm Eying Bigger Picture." *Toledo Blade* 18 April 1971.

———. "Toledo's Craft House helps boost parent into Fortune 500." *Toledo Blade,* 8 April 1994.

Brooks, Leonard. "You Too Can Paint." *Atlantic Monthly* 195 (June 1955): 86.

Brown, Ian. "Take a Number." *Globe and Mail* [Toronto, CN], 24 July 1999, sec. C, 1, 5.

Brown, V. K. "What Shall We Do with This New Leisure?" *Parks & Recreation* 17 (1934): 361–364; 18 (1934): 26–29.

Bruner, Louise. "The Figure Paintings of Adam Grant." *American Artist* 37 (January 1973): 24–27, 71.

Burnham, Sophie. *The Art Crowd.* New York: McKay, 1973.

Burns, Mark and Louis DiBonis. *Fifties Homestyle: Popular Ornament of the USA.* New York: Harper and Row, 1988.

"Business Boom for Young Promotion-Minded Firm." *Art Materials Trade News* (January 1954): 25, 36.

Butsch, Richard, ed. *For Fun and Profit: The Transformation of Leisure into Consumption.* Philadelphia: Temple University Press, 1990.

Butterworth, William. "New Leisure and a New Job for Management." *Factory Management and Maintenance* 92 (April 1934): 167–169.

Byerly, Florence. "See What You Can Do With Pictures!" *Better Homes and Gardens* 33 (June 1955): 84–85.

Caen, Herb. *San Francisco Examiner* 20 October 1952: 29.

Calkins, E. E. "The New Leisure: A Curse or a Blessing?" *Economic Forum* 1 (Fall 1933): 371–382.

Carter, Mary Randolph. *American Junk.* New York: Viking Penguin, 1994: 160–161.

Chase, Stuart. "Leisure in a Machine Age." *Library Journal* 56 (August 1931): 629–632.

"Churchill Art Rejected In Chicago as 'Amateur.'" *New York Times* 22 April 1958: 35

Churchill, Winston S. *Amid These Storms: Thoughts and Adventures.* New York: Charles Scribner's Sons, 1932.

Clark, Clifford Edward, Jr. *The American Family Home from 1800–1960.* Chapel Hill: University of North Carolina Press, 1986.

Clark, Clifford E. Jr. "Ranch House Suburbia: Ideals and Realities." In Lary May, ed. *Recasting America: Culture and Politics in the Age of Cold War.* Chicago: University of Chicago Press, 1989: 171–191.

Clarke, Alfred C. "Leisure and Occupational Prestige." In Eric Larrabee and Rolf Meyersohn, eds. *Mass Leisure.* New York: The Free Press, 1958: 205–214.

Clarke, John. "Pessimism vs. Populism: The Problematic Politics of Popular Culture." In Richard Butsch, ed. *For Fun and Profit: The Transformation of Leisure into Consumption.* Philadelphia: Temple University Press, 1990: 28–44.

Collins, Bradford. *Life* Magazine and the Abstract Expressionists, 1948–51: A Historiographic Study of a Late Bohemian Enterprise. *Art Bulletin* 73 (June 1991): 283–308.

Cook, Charles. "Art for Today's Child." *The School Arts Magazine* 56 (September 1956): 11–14.

Conant, John. "Creative Art Activities in a Viewer-Participation Type Television Program." *Art Education* 6 (January, 1953): 2–5.

"Conditions Promoting Desirable Growths." *Art Education* 6 (May 1953): 22–23.

Conn, Steven. *Museums and American Intellectual Life, 1876–1926.* Chicago: University of Chicago Press, 1998.

Coplans, John. "Early Warhol: The Systematic Evolution of the Impersonal Style." *Artforum* 8 (March 1970): 52–59.

Craven, David. "Abstract Expressionism, Automatism, and the Age of Automation." *Art History* 13 (March 1990): 72–103.

Cross, Gary. *Kids' Stuff: Toys and the Changing World of American Childhood.* Cambridge: Harvard University Press, 1997.

———. "The Suburban Weekend: Perspectives on a Vanishing 20th Century Dream." In Roger Silverstone, ed. *Visions of Suburbia.* London: Routledge, 1997: 108–132.

Daniels, Mary. "Count on It: Who Would Have Ever Thought Those Paint-by-Number Compositions Would Reach Gallery Status?" *Chicago Tribune* 12 September 1993, sec. 15, 3.

De Francesco, Italo L. "Art Education Then And Now." *The School Arts Magazine* 55 (April 1956): 5–12.

De Grazia, Sebastian. *Of Time, Work, and Leisure.* Hartford, CT: Connecticut Printers, Inc. 1962.

"Decorate to Enjoy Your Hobby More." *Better Homes and Gardens* 31 (October 1953): 214.

"Decorating Scrapbook." *Better Homes and Gardens* 28 (September 1949): 52–53.

d'Harnoncourt, Rene. "Challenge and Promise: Modern Art and Modern Society." *Magazine of Art* 41 (November 1948): 250–252.

Deitcher, David. "Unsentimental Education: The Professionalization of the American Artist." In Russell Ferguson, ed. *Hand-Painted Pop: American Art in Transition, 1952–1962.* Exhibition catalog. Los Angeles: Museum of Contemporary Art, 1992, 95–118.

Denney, Reuel. *The Astonished Muse.* Chicago: University of Chicago Press, 1957.

———. "Leisure in Industrial America." In Eugene Staley, ed. *Creating and Industrial Civilization.* New York: Harper & Bros., 1952: 245–281.

———. "The Leisure Society." *Harvard Business Review* 37 (May/June 1959): 46–60.

Denney, Reuel and David Riesman. "Leisure and Human Values in Industrial Civilization." In Eugene Staley, ed. *Creating an Industrial Civilization.* New York: Harper & Bros., 1952: 50–91.

Denney, Reuel and Mary Lee Meyersohn, comps. "A Preliminary Bibliography on Leisure." In *The Uses of Leisure,* special issue of *American Journal of Sociology* 62 (May 1957): 602–615.

De Voto, Bernard. "Why Professors Are Suspicious of Business." *Fortune* 43 (April 1951): 114–115, 139, 140, 142, 144.

Diggins, John. *The Proud Decades: America in War and Peace, 1941–1960.* New York: W.W. Norton, 1988.

"Do it with Pictures." *Home and Garden* 103 (January, 1953): 77–80.

Dobriner, William M. *Class in Suburbia.* Englewood Cliffs: Prentice-Hall, 1963.

Dobriner, William M. ed. *The Suburban Community.* New York: Putnam, 1958.

Dorfles, Gillo. *Kitsch: The World of Bad Taste.* New York: Dell Publishing Company, 1975.

Doss, Erika. *Benton, Pollock, and the Politics of Modernism: From Regionalism to Abstract Expressionism.* Chicago: University of Chicago Press, 1991.

Douglass, Paul F., John L. Hutchinson, and Willard C. Sutherland, eds. "Recreation in the Age of Automation." Special issue. *Annals of the American Academy of Political and Social Sciences* 313 (September 1957).

"Dramatize Your Walls." *Good Housekeeping* 139 (September 1954): 181B.

"Draw for Money! Be an Artist" (advertisement). *Popular Science* 156 (May 1950): 38.

Dunser, Anna. "Creative Art and Democracy." *The School Arts Magazine* 53 (May 1954): 29.

Edwards, Kim. "Telling it on the Mountain: Peggy Grant's quest to keep her husband's legacy alive." *Toledo City Paper* (August 1999): 46.

Eisenberg, Helen and Larry Eisenberg. *The Family Fun Book.* New York: Association Press, 1953.

Eisenhower, Dwight D. *At Ease: Stories I Tell to Friends.* New York: Doubleday & Co., 1967.

Ellison, Jerome "Anyone Can Paint a Picture." *Saturday Evening Post* 226 (December 19, 1953): 22–23.

Ewing, William L. *America Worked. The 1950s Photographs of Dan Weiner.* New York: Harry N. Abrams, 1989.

"The Executive Grabs His Paints." *Business Week* (April 14, 1951): 22–23.

Foster, Stephen C. "Early Pop and the Consumptive Critic. In Russell Ferguson, ed. *Hand-Painted Pop: American Art in Transition, 1952–1962.* Exhibition catalog. Los Angeles: Museum of Contemporary Art, 1992: 163–177.

Foy, Jessica H. and Karal Ann Marling, eds. *The Arts and the American Home, 1890–1930.* Knoxville, TN: University of Tennessee Press, 1994.

Frank, Thomas and Matt Weiland, eds. *Commodify Your Dissent: Salvos from the Baffler.* New York: W. W. Norton & Company, 1997.

Frankl, Paul T. *Machine-Made Leisure.* New York: Harper & Bros., 1932.

———. *New Dimensions.* New York: Brewer & Warren, Inc., 1928.

Frith, Simon and Howard Horne. *Art Into Pop.* London and New York: Methuen, 1987.

Galbraith, John Kenneth. *The Affluent Society.* New York: Houghton Mifflin Company, 1969.

Gans, Herbert J. "American Popular Culture and High Culture in a Changing Class Structure." *Prospects* 10 (1985): 17–37.

———. *The Levittowners: Ways of Life and Politics in a New Suburban Community.* New York: Columbia University Press, 1982; Pantheon Books, 1967.

———. *Popular Culture and High Culture: An Analysis and Evaluation of Taste.* New York: Basic Books, 1974.

Gardner, George, et al. "New Social Problem: Leisure Time." *School and Society* 42 (August 31, 1935): 294–296.

Gelber, Steven M. *Hobbies: Leisure and the Culture of Work in America.* New York: Columbia University Press, 1999.

Gitlin, Todd. "Mass Media Sociology: The Dominant Paradigm." *Theory and Society* 6 (September 1978): 205–253.

Goldstein, Carolyn M. *Do It Yourself: Home Improvement in 20th Century America.* New York: Princeton Architectural Press, 1998.

"Good Art in Good Prints." *Good Housekeeping* 129 (July 1949): 78.

"Good Grouping for Your Pictures." *Better Homes and Gardens* 32 (April 1954): 36.

Gotshalk, D. W. *Art and the Social Order.* New York: Dover Publications, Inc., 1962.

Grabar, Oleg. *The Mediation of Ornament.* Princeton, NJ: Princeton University Press, 1992.

Graftly, Dorothy. "Where the Public Buys Art." *American Artist* 19 (March 1955): 51–7.

Grant, Ila S. "Sage Brushings." Bend, Oregon *Bulletin* 24 March 1954.

Greenberg, Clement. "Abstract, Representational, and so forth" (1954). In Greenberg, *Art and Culture: Critical Essays.* Boston: Beacon Press, 1961: 133–138.

———. "'American-Type' Painting" (1955, 1958). In Greenberg, *Art and Culture: Critical Essays.* Boston: Beacon Press, 1961: 208–229.

———. "Avant Garde and Kitsch." *Partisan Review* 6 (Fall 1939): 34–49. In Greenberg, ed. *The Collected Essays and Criticism.* Vol. 1. *Perceptions and Judgments 1939–1944.* Chicago: University of Chicago Press, 1986: 5–22.

———. *Homemade Esthetics: Observations on Art and Taste.* New York: Oxford University Press, 1999.

———. "The Present Prospects of American Painting and Sculpture." 1947. In John O'Brian, ed. *The Collected Essays and Criticism.* Vol. 2. *Arrogant Purpose 1945–1949.* Chicago: University of Chicago Press, 1986: 160–170.

———. "Review of the Water-Color, Drawing, and Sculpture Sections of the Whitney Annual." 1946. In John O'Brian, ed. *The Collected Essays and Criticism.* Vol. 2. *Arrogant Purpose 1945–1949.* Chicago: University of Chicago Press, 1986: 57–59.

———. "Work and Leisure Under Industrialism: The Plight of Our Culture: Part II." *Commentary* 16 (July 1953): 54–62.

Greenbie, Sydney. *Leisure for Living.* New York: G. W. Stewart, 1940.

Grier, Katherine C. *Culture and Comfort: Parlor-Making and Middle Class Identity, 1850–1930.* Washington, D.C.: Smithsonian Institution Press, 1988.

Guilbaut, Serge. *How New York Stole the Idea of Modern Art: Abstract Expressionism, Freedom, and the Cold War.* Arthur Goldhammer, trans. Chicago: University of Chicago Press, 1983.

Graebner, William. *The Engineering of Consent: Democracy and Authority in Twentieth-Century America.* Madison: University of Wisconsin Press, 1987.

Guptill, Arthur L. "Those Ubiquitous Numbered Painting Sets." *American Artist* 17 (December 1953): 58–61.

Haddow, Robert H. *Pavilions of Plenty: Exhibiting American Culture Abroad in the 1950s.* Washington: Smithsonian Institution Press, 1997.

Halle, David. *America's Working Man: Work, Home, and Politics Among Blue-Collar Property Owners.* Chicago: University of Chicago Press, 1984.

———. *Inside Culture: Art and Class in the American Home.* Chicago: University of Chicago Press, 1993.

Halttunen, Karen. "From Parlor to Living Room: Domestic Space, Interior Decoration, and the Culture of Personality." In Simon Bronner, ed. *Consuming Visions: Accumulation and Display of Goods in America, 1880–1920.* New York: W. W. Norton, 1989.

Harris, Neil. "Museums, Merchandising, and Popular Taste: the Struggle for Influence." In I. M. G. Quimby, ed. *Material Culture and the Study of American Life.* New York: Norton, 1978: 140–174.

Hess, Alan. *Googie: Fifties Coffee Shop Architecture.* San Francisco: Chronicle Books, 1985.

"High-Brow, Low-Brow, Middle-Brow." *Life* 26 (April 11, 1949): 99–101.

Hine, Thomas. *Populuxe.* New York: Alfred A. Knopf, 1986.

Hofstadter, Richard. *Anti-intellectualism in American Life.* New York: Knopf, 1963.

Holbrook, Christine. "How To Build Color Schemes." *Better Home and Gardens* 28 (October 1949): 44.

Houseman, Robert W. "For Gifts—These Hobby Kits." *The American Home* 52 (October 1954): 118–120.

"How Do YOU Rate in the New Leisure? Russell Lynes, A Witty Observer, Charts a New Class System." *Life* 47 (December 28, 1959): 85–89.

"How to Hang Pictures." *McCalls* 80 (March 1953): 102–103.

Hunt, Herold C. "Art Helps Character." *The School Arts Magazine* 53 (January 1954): 5–6.

"It's Two-Faced and There's a Blueprint for It!" *The American Home* 52 (November 1954): 62–63.

Jackson, Kenneth T. *Crabgrass Frontier: The Suburbanization of the United States.* New York: Oxford University Press, 1985.

Jacobs, Norman, ed. *Culture for the Millions? Mass Media in Modern Society.* Princeton: D. Van Nostrand Company, Inc., 1959.

Jarrell, Randall. "A Sad Heart at the Supermarket." In Norman Jacobs, ed. *Culture for the Millions? Mass Media in Modern Society.* Princeton, NJ: D. Van Nostrand Company, Inc., 1959 and 1961.

Johnson, Victor. "Art World Battles: 'Numbers Racket' Gets Attention of Critics." *Grand Rapids Herald Magazine* (June 13, 1954): 8.

Johnson, W. H. "Education for Leisure." *Chicago Schools Journal* 7 (February 1925): 204–207.

Judy, Bernard. "Toledo Firm Cashing In On Growth of Paint-By-The-Numbers Hobby." *Toledo Blade* 26 October 1958.

Kahn, O. H. "Leisure and Art." *Peabody Journal of Education* 6 (November 1928): 131–144.

Kakutani, Michiko. "Portrait of the Artist As a Focus Group." *New York Times Magazine* (March 1, 1998): 26.

Kammen, Michael. *American Culture, American Tastes: Social Change and the Twentieth Century.* New York: Alfred A. Knopf, 1999.

Kasson, John F. *Amusing the Millions: Coney Island at the Turn of the Century.* New York: Hill and Wang, 1978.

Kaye, Marvin. *A Toy Is Born.* New York: Stein and Day, 1973.

Keats, John, *The Crack in the Picture Window.* New York: Ballantine Books, 1956.

Kelly, Barbara M. *Expanding the American Dream: Building and Rebuilding Levittown.* Albany: State University of New York Press, 1993.

Kimmelman, Michael. "Painting by Numbers: How Bad Was It?" *New York Times* 9 October 1994: sec. 2, 34.

King, Lt. William H. "Hobbyist in Bellbottoms." *The Hobby Merchandiser* 6 (October 1953): 28–29.

Klayman, Ben. "Craft House sale made." *Toledo Blade* 14 June 1997.

Klein, Max. "'The inside profit story of the paint-by-number business.'" *Toys and Novelties* 50 (July 1953): 16.

Knighton, Jr., William. "That's Washington." *Baltimore Sun* 14 October 1956: 19.

Knowlton, William H. "You, Too, Can Be an Artist!" *Sales Management* 71.1 (September 1, 1953): 126–129.

Kozloff, Max. "American Painting During the Cold War." *Artforum* 11 (May 1973): 43–54.

Kramer, Jane. *Whose Art Is It?* Durham, NC: Duke University Press, 1994.

Krames, Bill. "Turnover 'Quicks.'" *The Hobby Merchandiser* 6 (July 1953): 40.

Larrabee, Eric. "What's Happening to Hobbies?" In Eric Larrabee and Rolf Meyersohn, eds. *Mass Leisure*. New York: The Free Press 1958, pp. 268–274.

Larrabee, Eric and Rolf Meyersohn, eds. *Mass Leisure*. New York: The Free Press 1958.

Lears, Jackson. "A Matter of Taste: Corporate Cultural Hegemony in a Mass-Consumption Society." In Lary May, ed. *Recasting America: Culture and Politics in the Age of Cold War*. Chicago: University of Chicago Press, 1989: 38–57.

"Leisure and Aesthetics." *Nation* 108 (1919): 187.

"The Leisured Masses." *Business Week* (September 12, 1953): 142–152.

Leja, Michael. *Reframing Abstract Expressionism: Subjectivity and Painting in the 1940s*. New Haven: Yale University Press, 1993.

"Letters to the Editor." *American Artist* 17 (June 1953): 4.

Leuchtenburg, William. *The Perils of Prosperity, 1914–32*. Chicago: University of Chicago Press, 1958.

———. *A Troubled Feast: American Society Since 1945*. Boston, MA: Little, Brown and Co., 1983.

Levine, Lawrence W. *Highbrow/Lowbrow: The Emergence of Cultural Hierarchy in America*. Cambridge, MA: Harvard University Press, 1988.

Levine, Lawrence, Robin Kelley, Natalie Davis, and T. J. Jackson Lears. "AHR Forum: The Folklore of Industrial Society: Popular culture and Its Audiences." *American Historical Review* 97 (December 1992): 1369–1430.

Lewis, Howard J. "Sunday Painting . . . The Fad That Came to Stay." *Cleveland Plain Dealer This Week Magazine* (August 15, 1954): 8–9.

Lhamon, W. T. *Deliberate Speed: The Origins of a Cultural Style in the American 1950s*. Washington: Smithsonian Institution Press, 1990.

Lies, Eugene T. "The New Leisure: Drafting a Program." *New York Times Magazine* (December 3, 1933): 3, 32.

Lipsitz, George. *Class and Culture in Cold War America: "A Rainbow at Midnight."* South Hadley, MA: J. F. Bergin Publishers, 1981.

———. *Time Passages: Collective Memory and American Popular Culture*. Minneapolis: University of Minnesota Press, 1990.

"Little Picture Galleries." *Good Housekeeping* 139 (October 1954): 196.

Livingstone, Marco. "Do It Yourself: Notes on Warhol's Techniques." In Kynaston McShine. Ed. *Andy Warhol: A Retrospective*. New York: Museum of Modern Art distributed by Bullfinch Press/Little, Brown, 1989: 63–78.

Loran, Erle. "Pop Artists or Copycats?" *Art News* 62 (September 1963): 48–49, 61.

Lowenfeld, Viktor. "Creative Growth in Child Art." *Design* 56 (September 1954): 12–13.

Lunz, Lois M. "Personality and Publicity Put Palmer in First Place." *The Hobby Merchandiser* 6 (September1953): 32–35.

Lupton, Ellen. *Mechanical Brides: Women and Machines from Home to Office*. New York: Princeton Architectural Press, 1993.

Lynes, Russell. "Highbrow, Lowbrow, Middlebrow." *Harper's* 198 (February 1949): 19–28.

———. *The Tastemakers: The Shaping of American Popular Taste*. New York: Harper and Brothers; 1954; Dover Publications, 1980.

Lyons, E. "Menace of Leisure." *American Mercury* 48 (December 1939): 477–479.

MacIver, Robert. "The Great Emptiness." In MacIver, *The Pursuit of Happiness*. New York: Simon & Schuster, 1955.

Mamiya, Christin J. *Pop Art and Consumer Culture: American Supermarket*. Austin: University of Texas Press, 1992.

"Man for the Machine." *Time* 212 (May 24, 1971): 68–69.

Manzella, David. "Numbered Paintings, Player Pianos, and Love Potions." *The School Arts Magazine* 55 (June 1956): 24–26.

Marling, Karal Ann. *As Seen on TV: The Visual Culture of Everyday Life in the 1950s*. Cambridge: Harvard University Press, 1994.

———. *Norman Rockwell*. New York: Harry N. Abrams in association with the National Museum of American Art, Smithsonian Institution, 1997.

Marsh, Margaret. *Suburban Lives*. New Brunswick, NJ: Rutgers University Press, 1990.

Marzio, Peter C. *The Art Crusade: An Analysis of American Drawing Manuals, 1820–1860*. Washington: Smithsonian Institution Press, 1976.

———. *Mr. Audubon and Mr. Bein: Early Phase in the History of American Chromolithography*. Washington: Smithsonian Institution, 1975.

"Master Artist Materials" (advertisement). *The Hobby Merchandiser* 6 (June 1953): 68.

May, Elaine Tyler. *Homeward Bound: American Families in the Cold War Era*. New York: Basic Books, 1988.

Mayer, Marion M. "Of Course You Can Paint!" *The American Home* 50 (July 1953): 27–29.

McAfee, Helen. "Menace of Leisure: What to Do with the Sixteen-hour Day." *Century* 114 (1927): 67–76.

McClintock, Inez and Marshall McClintock. *Toys in America*. Washington: Public Affairs Press, 1961.

McCracken, Grant. *Culture and Consumption: New Approaches to the Symbolic Character of Consumer Goods and Activities*. Bloomington: Indiana University Press, 1990.

McKinzie, Richard D. *The New Deal for Artists*. Princeton: Princeton University Press, 1975.

McShine, Kynaston, ed. *Andy Warhol: A Retrospective*. New York: Museum of Modern Art distributed by Bullfinch Press/Little, Brown, 1989.

McMullen, Roy. "Some Pleasures and Problems of Modern Painting." *House Beautiful* 98 (October 1956): 192–193.

Mead, Margaret. "The Pattern of Leisure in Contemporary American Culture." In Eric Larrabee and Rolf Meyersohn, eds. *Mass Leisure*. New York: The Free Press, 1958: 10–14. Also in *Annals of the American Academy of Political and Social Science* 313 (September 1957): 11–15.

Meyersohn, Rolf with the assistance of Marilyn Marc. "A Comprehensive Bibliography on Leisure, 1900–1958." In Eric Larrabee and Rolf Meyersohn, eds. *Mass Leisure*. New York: The Free Press 1958: 389–419.

Meyersohn, Rolf and Elihu Katz. "Notes on a Natural History of Fads." In Eric Larrabee and Rolf Meyersohn, eds. *Mass Leisure*. New York: The Free Press, 1958: 305–315.

Mills, C. Wright. *The Power Elite*. New York: Oxford University Press, 1956.

———. *White Collar: The American Middle Classes*. New York: Oxford University Press, 1951, 1956.

Montgomery, Ruth. "D.C. Wash." New York *Daily News* 4 March 1955.

Moran, Lawrence. "The Myth of Machine-Made Leisure: Who Will Redefine Leisure?" *Social Order* 6 (1956): 434–439.

Morris, Sylvia Jukes. *Rage for Fame: The Ascent of Clare Boothe Luce*. New York: Random House, 1997.

Mukerji, Chandra and Michael Schudson. *Rethinking Popular Culture: Contemporary Perspectives in Cultural Studies*. Berkeley: University of California Press, 1991.

Mumford, Lewis. *The City in History*. New York: Harcourt, Brace, 1961.

Murray, Stuart and James McCabe. *Norman Rockwell's Four Freedoms: Images that Inspire a Nation*. Stockbridge, MA: Berkshire House Publishers, 1993.

"National Amateur Art Festival" (advertisement). *American Artist* 17 (March 1953): 73.

"National Amateur Festival . . . here it is!" *American Artist* 17 (May 1953): 36–37.

"The New Do-It-Yourself Market." *Business Week* (June 14, 1952): 60–76.

"The New Leisure Class." *Tide* 31 (April 12, 1957): 38–42.

"New Use for Number Sets." *The School Arts Magazine* 54 (March 1955): 29.

Newton, Eric. "Diagnosis of a New Disease: Amateur Paintitis." *New York Times Magazine* (September 25, 1949): 17, 34–35.

Nickles, Shelley K. "Object Lessons: Household Appliance Design and the American Middle Class, 1920–1960," Ph.D. dissertation, University of Virginia, 1999.

Nord, David Paul. "An Economic Perspective on Formula in Popular Culture." *Journal of Popular Culture* 3 (Spring 1980): 17–28.

Norton, Anne. *Republic of Signs: Liberal Theory and American Popular Culture.* Chicago: University of Chicago Press, 1993.

O'Connor, Francis. Comp. *Art for the Millions: Essays from the 1930s by Artists and Administrators of the WPA Federal Art Project.* Boston: New York Graphic Society, 1973.

O'Connor, Francis. Ed. *The New Deal Art Projects: An Anthology of Memoirs.* Washington, D.C.: Smithsonian Institution Press, 1972.

O'Donoghue, Michael. "A Head for Numbers." *House & Garden* 164 (November 1992): 74–76).

O'Neill, William. *American High: The Years of Confidence, 1945–1960.* New York: The Free Press, 1986.

Ostrow, Albert A. *Planning Your Home for Play.* Atlanta, GA: Tupper & Love, 1954.

"Paint-By-Numbers Fad Sweeping Nation; $80,000,000 Worth Sold." *The Register* [Santa Ana, CA] 3 May 1954, p. B7.

"Painting by Numbers: The Search for a 'People's Art.'" *The Nation* (March 14, 1994): 334–348.

"Painting by the Numbers." *San Francisco Chronicle* 7 September 1952: 1, 9L. Cf. Caen, Herb, October 1952.

"Painting Can Open Up a Whole New World for Your Child." *House and Garden* 107 (February, 1955): 46–47.

"Palmer-Pann Changes Name." *Toledo Blade* 21 October 1963.

Persico, Joseph E. *The Imperial Rockefeller: A Biography of Nelson A. Rockefeller.* New York: Simon and Schuster, 1987.

Polcari, Stephen. *Abstract Expressionism and the Modern Experience.* New York: Cambridge University Press, 1991.

Potter, David M. *People of Plenty: Economic Abundance and the American Character.* Chicago: University of Chicago Press, 1954.

Pound, A. "Education for Leisure." In Henry W. Holmes and Burton P. Fowler. The Path of Learning. Boston: Little, Brown & Co., 1926: 71–89.

"Prints to Collect." *Hobbies* 55 (October 1950): 28–29.

Radway, Janice. "Mail-Order Culture and Its Critics: The Book-of-the Month Club, Commodification and Consumption, and the Problem of Cultural Authority." In Lawrence Grossberg, Cary Nelson, and Paula Treicher. Eds. *Cultural Studies.* New York and London: Routledge, 1989.

Ramsy, John. "Decorative Prints." *Hobbies* 54 (May 1949): 26–27.

Reich, Cary. *The Life of Nelson A. Rockefeller: Worlds to Conquer, 1908–1996.* New York: Doubleday, 1996.

Riesman, David. *Abundance for What? And Other Essays.* New York: Doubleday, 1964.

———. "Leisure and Work in Post-Industrial Society." In Eric Larrabee and Rolf Meyersohn, eds. *Mass Leisure.* New York: The Free Press, 1958: 363–385.

———. "The Suburban Sadness." In William Dobriner, ed. *The Suburban Community.* New York: G. P. Putnam's Sons, 1958: 375–408.

Riesman, David, with Nathan Glazer and Reuel Denney. *The Lonely Crowd.* New Haven: Yale University Press, 1950.

Reynolds, Mary M'Donald. "It's by the Numbers." *Chattanooga Times* 16 May 1954.

Robbins, Dan. *Whatever Happened to Paint by Numbers?* Delavan, WI: Possum Hill Press, 1997.

The Nelson Rockefeller Collection. New York: Nelson Rockefeller, Inc., 1978.

Rohan, Barry. "A Brush with History: Troy Firm Restores the Fun of the '50s Paint-by-Number Sets." *Detroit Free Press* 19 January 1995, sec. D, 1–2.

Roland, Albert. "Do-It-Yourself: A Walden for the Millions?" *American Quarterly* 10 (Summer 1958): 154–164.

"Room to Enjoy the New Leisure." *House + Home* 5 (May 1954): 134–137.

Rosenberg, Bernard and David Manning White. Eds. *Mass Culture: The Popular Arts in America.* New York: The Free Press, 1957.

Rosenberg, Harold. "The American Action Painters." In *The Tradition of the New.* New York: Horizon Press, 1959.

———. *The Anxious Object: Art Today and Its Audience.* New York: Horizon Press, 1964.

Ross, Andrew. *No Respect: Intellectuals and Popular Culture.* New York and London: Routledge, 1989.

———. "Poll Stars." *ArtForum* (January 1995): 72–77, 109.

Ross, Clifford. Ed. *Abstract Expressionism: Creators and Critics.* New York: Harry N. Abrams, 1990.

Rossi, John. "Making It Big in the Numbers Racket! An Interview with 'Paint-by-Numbers Guru Dan Robbins.'" *Outre* no. 17 (1999): 26–31, 74–75.

Roszak, Theodore. *The Making of a Counter Culture: Reflections on the Technocratic Society and Its Youthful Opposition.* New York: Doubleday & Company, 1969.

Rubin, Joan Shelley. *The Making of Middlebrow Culture.* Chapel Hill: University of North Carolina Press, 1992.

Russell, Bertrand. "Leisure and Mechanism." *Dial* 75 (1923): 105–122.

Russel Sage Foundation. Library. *The New Leisure: Its Significance and Use.* New York: Russel Sage Foundation, 1933, rev. ed 1936.

Sargeant, Winthrop. "In Defense of the High-Brow." *Life* (April 11, 1949): 102.

Schjeldahl, Peter. "Barbarians at the Gate: The Triumph of Picabia and Warhol, in Two New Shows." *The New Yorker* (May 15, 2000): 103–104.

Seabrook, John. "Nobrow Culture." *The New Yorker* (September 20, 1999): 104–111.

"The Search for a People's Art." *The Nation* (March 14, 1994): 334–344+.

Shea, James J. as told to Charles Mercer. *It's All in the Game.* New York: G. P. Putnam's Sons, 1960.

Seiter, Ellen. *Sold Separately: Parents and Children in Consumer Culture.* New Brunswick, NJ: Rutgers University Press, 1993.

"Shell Your Own Corn." *Recreation* 47 (February 1954): 72.

Shi, David. *The Simple Life: Plain Living and High Thinking in American Culture.* New York: Oxford University Press, 1985.

Smith, Barbara Hernstein. "Contingencies of Value." In Robert von Hallberg, ed. *Canons.* Chicago: University of Chicago Press, 1984.

Smith, Janet K. "Art and the Homemaker." *Journal of Home Economics* 41 (November 1949): 497–498.

Smith, Patrick S. *Warhol: Conversations About the Artist.* Ann Arbor: UMI Research Press, 1988.

Smith, Pete. *The History of American Art Education.* Westport, CT: Greenwood Press, 1996.

Spigel, Lynn. "From Theatre to Space Ship." In Roger Silverstone, ed. Visions of Suburbia, London: Routledge, 1997: 215–239.

———. *Make Room for TV: Television and the Family Ideal in Postwar America.* Chicago: University of Chicago Press, 1992.

Spitzer, Leo. *A Method of Interpreting Literature.* Northampton, MA: Smith College, 1949; reprint ed., New York: Russell and Russell, 1967.

Solomon, Deborah. "Filling That Rectangle Above the Sofa." *New York Times* 19 March 1998: C11.

———. "In Praise of Bad Art." *New York Times Magazine* (January 24, 1999): 32–35.

Stewart, Jeffrey C. *To Color America: Portraits by Winold Reiss.* Washington, D.C.: Smithsonian Institution Press, 1989.

Stich, Sidra. "The Cultural Climate in America After World War II." In *Made in the USA: On Americanization in Modern Art, the 50s and 60s.* Berkeley: University of California Press, 1987: 6–13.

Stocker, Joseph. "BORED? Be A Happy Dabbler!" *Rotarian* 84 (April 1954): 15–17.

Stoner, Gerry. "You Can Own Masterpieces . . . at Down to Earth Prices." *Better Homes and Gardens* 28 (July 1950): 52–53.

Strauss, Anselm. *Images of the American City.* New York: The Free Press, 1961.

Susman, Warren I. *Culture as History: The Transformation of American Society in the Twentieth Century.* New York: Pantheon Books, 1984.

Sutton-Smith, Brian. *Toys As Culture.* New York: Gardner Press, 1986.

Stern, Sydney Ladensohn and Ted Schoenhaus. *Toyland: The High-Stakes Game of the Toy Industry.* Chicago: Contemporary Books, 1990.

Sutherland, Willard C. "A Philosophy of Leisure." *Annals of the American Academy of Political and Social Science* 313 (September 1957): 1–3.

Swados, Harvey. "Less Work, Less Leisure." In Eric Larrabee and Rolf Meyersohn, eds. *Mass Leisure.* New York: The Free Press, 1958: 353–363.

Swenson, G. R. "What Is Pop Art?: Answers from 8 Painters, Part I." *Artnews* 62 (November 1963): 24–27, 60–63.

Taubes, Fredric. "Random Thoughts On Subject Matter in Painting." *American Artist* 20 (May 1956): 31.

Tavel, Ronald. "Theatre of the Ridiculous." *Tri-Quarterly* 6 (Spring 1966): 92–109.

"These Fads have Built a Billion Dollar Business." *Business Week* (November 28, 1953): 78–86.

Thompson, Laura Amelia. *Workers' Leisure: A Select List of References.* Washington, D.C.: U. S. Government Printing Office, 1927.

"Through Craft Master Kits Award-Winning 'Sunday Artist' Guides Brushes of Thousands": 10–11.

Tichi, Cecelia. *Electronic Hearth: Creating An American Television Culture.* New York: Oxford University Press, 1991.

Toffler, Alvin. *The Culture Consumers: Art and Affluence in America.* New York: St. Martin's Press, 1964.

"Toledo Firm Bought By General Mills." *Toledo Blade* 6 September 1967.

Treanor, Aline Jean. "Know Numbers? Then Paint a Masterpiece." *Toledo Blade* 22 March 1953 sec. 5, 1.

"24 of the Finest Paintings " (Advertisement). *Better Homes and Gardens* 103 (February 1953): 21.

United States. Department of Commerce. "The Do-It-Yourself Market." In Eric Larrabee and Rolf Meyersohn, eds. *Mass Leisure.* New York: The Free Press, 1958: 274–281.

Vallongo, Sally. "Art by the Numbers: Former Toledoan's Amusing Memoir Adds to Resurgence of Interest in U.S. Phenomenon." *Toledo Blade (Toledo Magazine)* 16 May 1999: 6.

———. "Taking Art to the Source." *Toledo Blade,* 28 January 1998: 30, 33.

Van Matre, Lynn. "Paint-by-Numbers Now Popular Culture." *Chicago Tribune* 18 January 1999, sec. 2, p. 2.

Varnedoe, Kirk and Adam Gopnik. *High and Low: Modern Art and Popular Culture.* New York: Harry N. Abrams, 1990.

Veblen, Thorstein. *The Theory of the Leisure Class.* New York: New American Library, 1953; Macmillan, 1899.

Vernyi, Bruce. "Toledo: The Paint-By-Numbers Capital?" *Toledo Blade* 26 August 1984.

Warhol, Andy. *The Philosophy of Andy Warhol (From A to B and Back Again).* New York: Harcourt Brace and Company, 1975.

Warhol, Andy and Pat Hackett. *POPism: The Andy Warhol '60s.* New York: Harcourt Brace and Company, 1980.

Watson, Ernest W. "Poverty Amidst Plenty." *American Artist.* 18 (October 1954): 3.

Wattel, Harold L. "Levittown: A Suburban Community." In William Dobriner, ed. *The Suburban Community.* New York: G. P. Putnam's Sons, 1958: 287–313.

"Weekend Painting is Fun!" (advertisement). *Popular Science* 156 (January, 1950): 42.

Werner, Alfred. "The Painting Plague: Self Expression on Sunday." *The American Mercury* 75 (December 1952): 49–56.

Weschler, Herman J. "Blessed Be the Sunday Painter-May His Tribe Increase." *House & Garden* 102 (August 1952): 69, 85.

White, David Manning. Ed. *Pop Culture in America.* Chicago: Quadrangle Books, 1970.

Whyte, William H. Jr. *The Organization Man.* New York: Simon and Schuster, 1956.

Winebrenner, D. Kenneth. "Creative Citizens." *The School Arts Magazine* 54 (May 1955): 48.

———."Let Them Make Mistakes." *The School Arts Magazine* 53 (March 1954): 48.

———. "Numbers Nonsense." *The School Arts Magazine* 53 (January 1954): 4.

———. "Peeping Toms and Copy Cats" *The School Arts Magazine* 56 (December 56): 48.

———. "Process or Product." *The School Arts Magazine* 53 (June 1954): 48.

———."Teaching Tricks." *The School Arts Magazine* 56 (September 1956): 48.

———. "We Need Each Other." *The School Arts Magazine* 55 (February 1956): 48.

———. "What Makes It Art?" *The School Arts Magazine* 55 (December 1955): 48.

Winston, M. C. "The New Leisure." *Progressive Education* 4 (October – December 1927): 315–317.

Wolfe, Tom. *The Painted Word.* New York: Farrar, Straus and Giroux, 1975.

Wygant, Foster. *School Art in American Culture, 1820–1970.* Cincinnati, OH: Interwood Press, 1993.

Wypijewski, JoAnn, ed. *Painting By Numbers: Komar and Melamid's Scientific Guide to Art.* New York: Farrar, Straus & Giroux, 1997.

Yenawine, Philip, Marianne Weems, and Brian Wallis, eds. *Art Matters: How the Culture Wars Changed America.* New York: New York University Press, 1999.

"You Can Be A Famous Artist!" (advertisement). *Popular Science* (October 1950): 55.

Zeisel, Joseph, S. "The Workweek in American Industry, 1850–1956." In Eric Larrabee and Rolf Meyersohn, eds. *Mass Leisure.* New York: The Free Press, 1958, pp. 145–153.

ENDPAPER (FRONT). **Active Leisure**. *Life* 47 (December 28, 1959): 86–87. © 1959 Time, Inc. All rights reserved. SI #2000-3340.

ENDPAPER (REAR). **Sedentary Leisure**. *Life* 47 (December 28, 1959): 88-89. © 1959 Time, Inc. All rights reserved. SI #2000-3339.

FRONTISPIECE. **Statue of Liberty**. Testor's Master Palette, No. 402. 14 x 18". Lent by Trey Speegle SI #2000-4898.

INTRODUCTION

2. **Winter Snow**. 8 x 10" PBN/NMAH SI #2000-1395.

3. **Winter Snow**. Line art. 9 x 11". Paint by Number Collection, NMAH Archives Center, gift of Jacquelyn Schiffman (hereafter PBN/NMAH) SI #2000-1423.

4. **Paint-A-Player**. 6 3/4 x 10 1/2 x 1". Lent by Ed Derwent SI #2000-4885-02.

5 TOP LEFT. **Duke Snider**. 12 x 9". Lent by June Mersky SI #2000-6208.

5 TOP RIGHT. **Carl Erskine**. 12 x 9". Lent by June Mersky SI #2000-1526.

5 BOTTOM LEFT. **Bob Lemon**. 12 x 9". Lent by Roger Bruns SI #2000-4896.

5 BOTTOM CENTER. **Bobby Avila**. 12 x 9". Lent by Roger Bruns SI #2000-4900

5 BOTTOM RIGHT. **Larry Doby**. 12 x 9". Lent by Roger Bruns SI #2000-4901

6. **Schematic diagram illustrating paint by number technique**. Palmer Paint. PBN/NMAH SI #2000-1410.

7 LEFT. **Twin Scotty paint kit**. Master Artists Materials, Inc. 13 1/4 x 12 1/4 x 1 1/4". Lent by Larry Rubin SI #2000-4883-02.

7 RIGHT. **Masterpiece oil painting set**. Palmer Paint. 10 x 20 x 1 1/2". Lent by Larry Rubin SI #2000-4887-01.

8 TOP LEFT. **Picture Craft oil painting set**. Picture Craft. 4 x 14 x 2". Lent by Ed Derwent SI #2000-4887-02, also 2000-4879.

8 TOP RIGHT. **Mountain Road**. Picture Craft. 12 x 16". Lent by Dan Robbins SI #2000-4867

8 BOTTOM RIGHT. **Columbia Jay**. Picture Craft. 16 x 12 x 1". Lent by Trey Speegle SI #2000-4899

9. **Desert Landscape**. Picture Craft. 12 1/2 x 15". Lent by Ed Derwent SI #2000-4864.

10 LEFT. **3-D Picture Paint by Number**. Pressman. 12 1/4 x 18 1/4 x 2 1/2". Lent by Larry Rubin SI #2000-4875.

10 RIGHT. **Master Palette Alphabetically Keyed Oil Painting Kit**. Testors. 10 1/4 x 14 1/4 x 1". Lent by Larry Rubin SI # 2000-4876.

11. *The Crack in the Picture Window*. 1956. SI #2000-5099.

12 LEFT. **Autumn Gold**. Craft Master M-319. 18 x 24". Lent by June Mersky SI #2000-6522

12 RIGHT. **Angler's Secret**. Craft Master, Palmer Pann New Artist Series 30 NA-3062. 20 x 16" Anon. SI #2000-4860.

13 LEFT. **Wall clock**. 9 x 7 1/2 x 2". Lent by John Donofrio SI #2000-4905

13 RIGHT. **More time for this**. Detroit Edison, c. 1955. Courtesy of Dan Robbins SI #2000-5085.

14. **Indian chief**. 18 x 8". Lent by Ed Derwent SI #2000-4865.

15. **Indian princess**. 18 x 8". Lent by Ed Derwent SI #2000-4866.

16. **Judaica**. 12 x 9". Lent by June Mersky SI #2000-4903.

17 LEFT. **Buddha**. 20 x 16". Anon. SI #2000-6517.

17 RIGHT. **Oriental Shrine**. Craftint King Size Deluxe Set KS-3. 18 x 24". Anon. SI #2000-4862.

18–19. **Christ in Gethsemane**. Craftint Big 3 Series C-1. 8 x 16". Lent by Trey Speegle SI #2000-4897.

52 TOP RIGHT. **Plus profit.** PBN/NMAH SI #2000-1403.

52 BOTTOM. **Shipping Department, Palmer Paint Co.** PBN/NMAH SI #2000-1435.

53. **Woolworth Annual Report for 1953.** PBN/NMAH SI #2000-1442.

CHAPTER TWO: THE NEW LEISURE

56. **Journey thru Space.** Craft Master CM 25. 12 x 16". Lent by Larry Rubin SI #2000-4888-03.

58 LEFT. **Journey thru Space (small).** Craft Master CM 25. 5 x 4". Lent by Larry Rubin SI #2000-4870.

58 RIGHT. **Journey thru Space (small).** Craft Master CM 25. 5 x 4" Lent by Larry Rubin SI #2000-4906.

59. **What happens to your job.** 1949. Records of the American Heritage Foundation, box 210 RG 200. Courtesy of the National Archives at College Park.

60. **"How Do YOU Rate in the New Leisure?"** *Life* (12/28/59): 85 ©1959 Time, Inc. All rights reserved. SI #2000-3341.

61. **Levittown, New York.** 1948. NMAH Division of Social History / Domestic Life Collection. Gift of Dr. Theodore and Ruth Finestone SI #2000-3336.

62 LEFT. **Balcony Ballet.** Craft Master New Artist Series 24 NA 2401. 16 x 12" Anon. SI #2000-4884-03.

62 RIGHT. **Balcony Ballet.** Craft Master New Artist Series 24 NA 2401. 16 x 12" Anon. SI #2000-4880-03.

63 TOP. **Gallery installation attributed to the Stix, Baer & Fuller department store, St. Louis.** PBN/NMAH SI #2000-1462.

63 BOTTOM LEFT. **Under the Bridge.** Craft Master M-310. 18 x 24". Lent by Trey Speegle SI #2000-4891.

63 BOTTOM RIGHT. **Oriental Beauty.** Craft Master M-313. 24 x 18". Lent by Ed Derwent SI #2000-4858.

64 TOP. **Trade show demonstrator.** PBN/NMAH SI #2000-1451.

64 BOTTOM. **Exhibit installation, Michigan Theater.** PBN/NMAH SI #2000-1408.

65. **Siesta in Mexico.** Craft Master CM 7. 16 x 12". Lent by Larry Rubin SI #2000-4869.

66 LEFT. **Artmobile.** PBN/NMAH SI #2000-1463.

66 RIGHT. **Artmobile interior.** PBN/NMAH SI #2000-3335.

67 TOP LEFT. **Toleware by Craft Master.** PBN/NMAH SI #2000-1440.

67 TOP RIGHT. **Toleware magazine rack.** Palmer Paint Co. NMAH Division of Social History, Domestic Life Collection gift of Jacquelyn Schiffman SI #2000-4889.

67 BOTTOM LEFT. Adam Grant. **Parisian series café scene.** Lent by the Popular Culture Library, Bowling Green State University.

67 BOTTOM RIGHT. Adam Grant. **Parisian series café scene.** Lent by the Popular Culture Library, Bowling Green State University.

68 LEFT. **Mosaic pixie.** 17 x 7" Anon. SI #2000-4885-01.

68 RIGHT. **Mosaic pixie.** 17 x 7" Anon. SI #2000-4888-01.

69 LEFT. **Mosette by Craft Master.** Palmer Paint Co. 7 1/2 x 13 x 1 1/2". Lent by Larry Rubin SI #2000-4882-03.

69 RIGHT. **Tile 'N Frame.** Palmer Paint Co. NMAH Ceramics and Glass Collection. Gift of Jacquelyn Schiffman SI #2000-4873.

70. **You Too Can Paint.** *Atlantic Monthly* 195 (June 1955): 86. SI # 2000-5102.

71. **Currier & Ives Pictures to Color.** 11 x 16 x 1 1/4". Lent by Larry Rubin SI #2000-4884-01.

72. **You Can Paint A Beautiful Picture.** Courtesy of Dan Robbins SI # 2000-5094.

73. **Van Gogh's The Bridge.** (Craft Master BRS-300 pre-embossed numbered oil painting set) 16 x 20". Lent by Trey Speegle SI #2000-6510.

76 TOP. **The Stephens Collection.** Courtesy of Mary Caffrey Stephens SI #2000-7167.

76 BOTTOM. **The Old Mill, signed Ethel Merman.** Craftint Big 3 Series D-1. Courtesy of Dwight D. Eisenhower Library.

77 TOP LEFT. **Old Mission completed by Nelson Rockefeller.** Picture Craft. Courtesy of Dwight D. Eisenhower Library.

77 TOP RIGHT. Clare Boothe Luce. **Black Child.** Watercolor. Courtesy of Dwight D. Eisenhower Library.

78. **Swiss Village completed by J. Edgar Hoover.** Picture Craft. Courtesy of Dwight D. Eisenhower Library.

79. **Avalon First Prize.** 11 x 15 3/4 x 1 1/2". Lent by Larry Rubin. SI #2000-4888-02.

80 LEFT. **New Use for Number Sets.** *The School Arts Magazine* 54 (March 1955): 29. Courtesy of Dr. Howard Conant. SI # 2000-5100.

80 RIGHT. **Playmates.** GS-1854 Craft Master Gallery Series II. 14 x 10". Lent by Larry Rubin. SI #2000-4880-01.

81 LEFT. **There Oughta Be A Law.** Courtesy of Dan Robbins. SI #2000-5095.

81 RIGHT. **Woman completing a child's "personal portrait."** PBN/NMAH SI #2000-1456.

82. **Lighthouse.** Picture Craft. with painted frame. 12 x 16". Lent by Jamie Owen SI #2000-4914.

83. **Yacht Race.** Picture Craft. with painted frame. 12 x 16". Lent by Jamie Owen SI #2000-6209.

84. **Winter Shadows.** Craftint King Size Deluxe #KS-1. 18 x 24". Lent by Ed Derwent. SI #2000-4859.

85. **Winter Shadows.** Craftint King Size Deluxe #KS-1 **without car.** 18 x 24". Lent by Jamie Owen SI #2000-6204.

CHAPTER THREE: THE PICTURE'S PLACE

88. **Floral still life signed Shirley Rae Roll.** 1953. 11 1/2 x 16". Lent by Gregory Brackens SI #2000-6512.

90. **Try these decorative ways to hang pictures.** Courtesy Larry Rubin SI #2000-7163.

91. **Day-to-Day family relationships.** Testors. Courtesy Larry Rubin SI #2000-7165.

92 LEFT. **Floral still life with figure.** Lent by Jamie Owen SI #2000-4911.

92 RIGHT. **Floral still life with deer figure.** Lent by Jamie Owen SI #2000-4909.

93 LEFT. **"Dinner is all ready . . . "** PBN/NMAH SI #2000-1461.

93 RIGHT. **Hibiscus in Bloom.** Craft Master M-311. 18 x 24". Lent by Trey Speegle SI #2000-6519.

94 TOP LEFT. **Snow covered village.** Lent by Jamie Owen SI#2000-4916.

94 TOP CENTER, BACK FLAP. **Snow scape boy with sled**. 12 x 16". Lent by Jamie Owen SI #2000-4913.

94 TOP RIGHT. **Snow scape (with church)**. 12 x 16". Lent by Jamie Owen SI #2000-4915 SI#2000-4915.

94 MIDDLE LEFT. **Rock, Surf and Sky**. Lent by Jamie Owen SI #2000-4912.

94 MIDDLE CENTER. **Swiss Village**. Craft Master M-309. 18 x 23". Lent by Trey Speegle. SI #2000-6524.

94 MIDDLE RIGHT. **After the Snow**. GS-2457 Craft Master Gallery Series III, professionally framed. 12 x 16". Anon. SI #2000-4881-02.

94 BOTTOM LEFT. **Fall Landscape**. Anon. SI#2000-4863.

94 BOTTOM RIGHT. **Vantage Point**. Super Craft Master SM-401. Lent by June Mersky SI #2000-6525.

95. **Conflict of the Sea**. Super Craft Master SM-405. 27 x 36". Lent by Trey Speegle SI #2000-4908.

96 LEFT. **Here's the answer to recreational problems on every post**. PBN/NMAH SI #2000-1404.

96 RIGHT. **Oriental Serenade**. Craft Master CM-28. 16 x 12". Lent by June Mersky SI #2000-6207.

97 LEFT. **Swan Lake Ballet**. Testors Master Palette No. 408. 16 x 20". Lent by Trey Speegle SI #2000-4892.

97 RIGHT. **Snowy Egrets**. Craftint King Size Deluxe #KS-7. 18 x 24". Lent by Jamie Owen SI #2000-6205.

98–99. **Indian Summer**. Super Craft Master SM-404. 27 x 36". Lent by Gregory Brackens SI #2000-6530.

EPILOGUE: THE UNFINISHED WORK

102. **Poling**. Craftint 400-S. 1959. A partially-painted paint by number image, printed on canvas board.

Image of a figure boating in a bayou. 12 x 16". Courtesy of The Archives of The Andy Warhol Museum, Pittsburgh; Founding Collection, Contribution The Andy Warhol Foundation for the Visual Arts, Inc.

104 LEFT. **Fun for the Entire Family**. Testor's. Courtesy of Larry Rubin. SI # 2000-5096.

104 RIGHT. **Deluxe Hobby Craft Series**. Hassenfeld Bros. 14 x 22 1/4 x 1 1/2". Lent by Larry Rubin SI #2000-4887-03.

105 LEFT. **Max Klein (left) and associates examining a mosaic table**. PBN/NMAH SI #2000-1417.

105 RIGHT. **Jumbo Planter Boxes**. PBN/NMAH SI #2000-1406.

106. **Still Life**. GS-3058 Craft Master Gallery Series IV Washington. Lent by Gregory Brackens SI #2000-6526.

107. **Still Life**. GS-3058 Craft Master Gallery Series IV Lincoln. Lent by Gregory Brackens SI #2000-6516.

108 LEFT. **Venus Paradise 4 Pre-Sketched Drawings**. Venus Pen & Pencil Corporation. Commercial package for Venus Paradise pencil-by-number kit "General Series Number 149-P-9." Verso used as a palette by Andy Warhol. No date, ca. early 1960s. 10 x 14 inches, courtesy of The Archives of The Andy Warhol Museum, Pittsburgh; Founding Collection, Contribution The Andy Warhol Foundation for the Visual Arts, Inc.

108 RIGHT. **Coastal Scene**. Venus Pen & Pencil Corporation. Source image for Warhol's painting *Do It Yourself (Seascape)*, 1963. A pencil by number image titled "Coastal Scene," publisher's model number 152-11, with pencilled notes. 9 1/2 x 13 1/4 inches, courtesy of The Archives of The Andy Warhol Museum, Pittsburgh; Founding Collection, Contribution The Andy Warhol Foundation for the Visual Arts, Inc.

109. Andy Warhol. **Do-it-Yourself (Seascape)**. Synthetic polymer paint and Prestype on canvas. 1963. 54" x 6'. Courtesy Heiner Bastian.

110 TOP. Andy Warhol. **Do-it-Yourself (Narcissus)**. 1962. Pencil and colored pencil on paper. 23 x 18". Courtesy Öffentliche Kunstsammlung Basel.

110 BOTTOM LEFT. Andy Warhol. **Do It Yourself (Flowers)**. 1962. Colored crayon on paper, 25 x 18". Lent by The Sonnabend Collection.

110 BOTTOM RIGHT. Andy Warhol. **Do-it-Yourself (Flowers)**. 1962. Synthetic polymer paint and Prestype on canvas. 69 x 59". Courtesy The Daros Collection.

111 LEFT. Andy Warhol. **Do-it-Yourself (Sailboats)**. 1962. Acrylic paint and Prestype on canvas. 72 x 100". Courtesy The Daros Collection

111 RIGHT. Andy Warhol. **Do-it-Yourself (Landscape)**. 1962. Synthetic polymer paint and Prestype on canvas. 70 x 54". Courtesy Museum Ludwig, Cologne

112. *Esquire* **magazine cover art**. Richard Hess. 1967. Courtesy of Samuel N. Antupit.

113. Paul Bridgewater. **Abstract Paint by Number Kit: Against the Looking Glass**. Unstretched canvas with accompanying typed instruction sheet. 1978. 34 x 40 3/4". Lent by the Andy Warhol Foundation.

115. **40 Years of Paint-by-Number Paintings**. 1992. 8 x 5_". Courtesy of Trey Speegle SI #2000-3330.

116 TOP. Vitaly Komar and Alex Melamid. **America's Most Wanted**. 1994. Acrylic on canvas. Dishwasher size. Courtesy of Vitaly Komar and Alex Melamid.

117 LEFT. Vitaly Komar and Alex Melamid. **People's Choice Color Preferences**. 1994. Acrylic on canvas. 48 x 60". Courtesy of Vitaly Komar and Alex Melamid.

117 RIGHT. Vitaly Komar and Alex Melamid. **America's Least Wanted**. 1994. Acrylic on canvas. Paperback size. Courtesy of Vitaly Komar and Alex Melamid.

ACKNOWLEDGMENTS

The production of an exhibit is by nature a collaborative and a collegial enterprise. The legitimacy of an exhibit is a function of the things in it. The gift collection of Jacquelyn Schiffman, the daughter of the late Max Klein, who donated her father's Palmer Paint Company scrapbooks and trade materials to the Museum, set me to thinking about such a show, and what it might hope to achieve. Dan Robbins generously made available his personal collection, including his infamous prototype for *Abstract No. 1*. Peggy Grant shared her reminiscences about work in the early days of Palmer Paint, and helped identify many of the artists involved. John A. Donofrio, Paul Kolasinski, and Harley Copic shared key information about the company's subsequent sale and purchase, and its paint kits in later years. Painting collectors Trey Speegle, Greg Brackens, Ed Derwent, Larry Rubin, June Mersky, Charles Levy, Flavio Belli, Jamie Owen, and Roger Bruns made their collections available for the asking. Dennis Medina of the Eisenhower Library, Matt Wrbican of the Andy Warhol Museum, Ileana Sonnabend of Sonnabend Gallery, Claudia Defendi of the Andy Warhol Foundation for the Visual Arts, and Alison M. Scott of the Popular Culture Library at Bowling Green State University generously lent their time and expertise to the project, as well as key materials from their respective collections. Paul Bridgewater provided background information about his adaptation of the paint by number motif; Mark Hess and Samuel N. Antupit shared their insights into the career of Richard Hess; Robert B. Sanders provided materials about the Picture Craft Company; Mary Caffery Stephens provided timely information and material describing the Stephens Collection; Howard S. Conant contributed a reminiscence and a clipping about his "new use" for number sets; Eric Enders of the National Baseball Hall of Fame Library assisted with ballplayer identification; and the librarians of the Toledo Public Library and the Cleveland Public Library mined local business history clipping files for materials documenting the respective activities of the Craft House Corporation and the Picture Craft Company. The hospitality of Mark Bello in Chicago, Greg Holman in Toronto, and Barry M. Landau in New York made collections research in and around those cities as fun as it was profitable.

A travel-to-collections grant awarded by the Office of Curatorial Affairs, National Museum of American History (NMAH) hastened the development of the exhibit idea. Along with the gentle guidance of the NMAH Exhibit and Program Committee, I wish to acknowledge the kind consideration and support of Spencer Crew, Martha Morris, Dennis S. Dickinson, Elizabeth Perry, Lonnie Bunch, Harold Closter, Jim Gardner, Hal Aber, Melinda Machado, John McDonagh, Anna Lincoln Whitehurst, and Cortney Powell.

The exhibit's thoughtful design and production is the distinct contribution of designer Constantine Raitzky, project manager Kathryn Campbell, editor Rosemary Regan, and team members Stevan Fisher, Marcia Powell, Carolyn Long, Joan Young, Sue Walther, Omar Wynn, and Tom Tearman.

I also wish to acknowledge the kind support of my colleagues in the NMAH Division of Social History: Susan Myers, the late Rodris Roth, Barbara Clark Smith, William Yeingst, Jennifer Oka, Bonnie Lilienfeld, Carol Kregloh, Priscilla Wood, Barbara Janssen, Doris Bowman, Shelly Foote, Harry R. Rubenstein, Lisa Kathleen Graddy, Marilyn Higgins, and Sandra Matthews; the NMAH Archives Center: Vanessa Broussard, Craig Orr, Wendy Shay, Robert Harding, and John Fleckner; the NMAH Branch Library: Jim Roan, Helen Holley, Stephanie Thomas, and Rhoda Ratner; and Joan Stahl of the National Museum of American Art library.

Early in the life of the exhibit idea, a survey of NMAH visitors' tastes in paintings elicited reminiscences about paint by number. The Smithsonian's Institutional Studies Office devised the survey, lead by Zahava Doering, Andy Pekarik, David Karns, Steven J. Smith, Abigail Dreibelbis, and Kerry DiGiacomo.

The clarity and beauty of the color catalog photography is the distinct contribution of the Smithsonian's Office of Printing and Photographic Services: Laurie H. Aceto, Harold Dorwin, Terry McCrea, Larry Gates, Dane Penland, Joe A. Goulait, and John Dolliver.

The specialists of the NMAH Office of Registration Services arranged for the safe transportation and documentation of loans, carried out by Batja Bell, Ed Ryan, Tom Bower, Kelly Ford, Margaret Grandine, Lynn Gilliland, and Katie Speckart.

The realization of this exhibit and catalog was made possible in ways large and small by the kind consideration of my colleagues Jessica Csoma, Catherine Wolfe, Helena Wright, David K. Allison, Rayna Green, Ellen Hughes, Marvette Perez, Harry Rand, Pete Daniel, Barney Finn, Arthur P. Molella, Steve Lubar, and Regina Blaszczyk.

Jennifer Noelle Thompson and Sara Stemen, my editors at Princeton Architectural Press, and my readers Erika Doss, Karal Ann Marling, Charles F. McGovern, Keith E. Melder, Shelley Nickles, Anne L. Pierce, and Roy Rosenzweig gave careful thought and attention to the manuscript, and saved me from glaring errors, omissions and interpretive lapses. Any that remain are mine.

WLB, JR.
Washington, D.C.